Learning Wing Chun Kung Fu

A step by step reference guide

Sifu Jason G. Kokkorakis

Published 2013 by arima publishing

www.arimapublishing.com

ISBN 978 1 84549 587 9

Printed and bound in the United Kingdom

Typeset in Garamond

arima publishing
ASK House, Northgate Avenue
Bury St Edmunds, Suffolk IP32 6BB
t: (+44) 01284 700321

www.arimapublishing.com

I have been fortunate enough to train with and learn from some of the most committed, talented and knowledgeable martial artists, during my thirty plus years of training. Obsessed with the detail, I am always looking to give an in depth feel and explanation of technique in my classes to benefit the students. Understanding detail gives you freedom and cuts through the mystical. Wing Chun is a highly practical approach to combat and is a worthy martial arts practice that anyone can apply themselves to. It is a simple formula, which I have now put into an order I can easily understand. This book is the first third of this formula, I hope it helps.

Acknowledgements

I would like to thank the following for their inspiration, teaching and sharing skills with me over the 23 years that I have been practicing Wing Chun. Sifu Colin Ward, Sifu Eddie Yuen, Sifu Clive Potter, Sifu Frank Grispos, Sifu Pedro Acha, Sifu Cheung Kwok Chow, Sifu David Peterson, Sifu Benny Meng, Sifu Suki Wan and Alan Gibson. Special thanks also to Grandmaster Samuel Kwok for his continued teachings and technical advice on Ip Man Wing Chun.

I would also like to thank my parents, for their love and constant support and my family, that I don't spend enough time with. Big thanks also to Scott Murray for the photos, Polly Fotheringham for the illustrations, Aaron Butcher, Adam Jones, Tom Keyworth, Daniel Christie, Heng Zhu and Neil Ashworth for their modelling services, and my long suffering partner Becky. Finally thanks to all my great students for their dedication and continued support of our school, and their appreciation of this amazing martial art.

In memory of Great Grandmaster Ip Man.

The fighting arts have evolved from the efforts of great martial art masters, warriors and teachers that saw a necessity to create systems of combat that could be learned and applied quickly and effectively, to protect themselves and their peoples. They have dedicated their lives understanding these things, and leave their legacy for us all to learn and develop from. We should use what has been contemplated, practiced and refined, as a guide to further self improvement and further development of these skills. If we do this, we all progress and cultivate ourselves and our bonds with each other, as well as further develop the system we practice, for future generations.

The Legend of Yim Wing Chun.

A young woman learns to fight in order to repel a gang leader's advances, as he wants to take her as his bride. Within a year of learning a new fighting skill, she meets him and beats him in a fight. If you take the story of her plight on its merits, you are talking about someone that has the inherent disadvantage of height, weight, strength and possibly attitude to fight. With the odds heavily stacked against you, how would you defeat the adversary?

Contents

Introduction

As a martial arts teacher and enthusiast of over thirty years, I can tell you, the path of martial knowledge is a very rewarding one to follow. It has been my obsession for over three decades, to find the way to true mastery in the best martial skills. This book details my journey of understanding. It is full of exercises and concepts that are realistic, efficient and practical. It is presented without the boundaries of lineage, tradition, myth or spirituality. Any good instructor will slowly expose you to the information contained in this book, but as you may not have access to one, this book is a good substitute for one to one instruction. Everything in this book, I and my students practice, for hundreds of hours, try and do the same. Form an opinion after you acquire all the skills, have worked them hard, and seen what they have done for you.

I will go into some detail on the forms, offering an insight into technical application of the movements, this will be focused more on the first two-forms but I will include some basics points on the others, including the weapons. I do however want to present a deeper explanation as to why a movement is performed and how it can be applied in practice. I hope you will take the information on board without ego, hostility or prejudice. It is after all, shared with you in order to help you achieve greater things in your training. Please take what is useful to you, and ignore the rest. Above all, enjoy practicing it.

Why Study Wing Chun?

Wing Chun is a concept based system of fighting theory that once understood, can be applied to any style, method or approach, therefore it is without limitation. Whatever you currently practice, you can use its theory to improve your skills.

The one problem most of us face, when learning to fight, is being comfortable at close proximity to aggressive force and attitude. Wing Chun develops fighting skill predominately at this range. It gives you in real terms, confidence to move into an aggressor and control them. Working with different training partners develops this in an unrehearsed and fluid way that is as varied in application and approach as the experience and attitudes of the people you practice with. They all offer a different challenge that the system slowly and methodically teaches you to overcome.

If you are not aggressive by nature, you can still learn to apply Wing Chun fully and effectively, being capable of all its concepts if your life depended on it, the survival instinct will guide your learned action. You only need to focus and commit yourself to learning its doctrine. Even at its most basic, the system offers the simplest and most practical way for people to learn to protect themselves effectively. It can be learned, understood and applied relatively quickly and the practitioner can defend themselves in a typical scenario after a reasonably short period of training.

It is also an incredibly safe way to exercise, there is no demand on overexertion, or performing separate stretching and exercise routines that could cause you physical problems later in life. All exercise is based on a common sense approach to combat, keeping you fit, alert and active. There is no better way to learn true fighting skill without ever having to fight. You can train for your entire life and never suffer injury, yet you will become a strong, physically and mentally able fighter.

The syllabus contains practical forms and drills, that act to build your skill in an attainable and well thought out way. The information blends together as a cohesive set of principles with each form building on from the other, developing further skills sets and principles that develop the practitioner.

How long does it take to be "Good"?

It's really down to you. As a practitioner, you must do exactly that, practice. Dedication, diligence, patience, persistence and commitment to training inside and outside of your school will make you a successful martial arts exponent.

Think on and understand why you are doing what you are doing in practice and constantly focus on improvement of your application, be patient and enjoy the learning process. If you see a technique for the first time and try to perform it as fast or smoothly as the expert, you may never get it right. Always break the technique down to individual parts and learn the detail, the stages of applications and the feel for the movement, as you improve, your ability to apply the action in reality will increase, take small steps.

Martial Arts & Reality

You must be clear about your intention when learning a fighting skill. Your first goal will be to learn to create solid defensive skills. Your second goal, to learn to develop realistic offensive skills, and then to combine them. Good defensive skill will give you greater opportunity to escape a conflict situation, good offensive skill will give you greater opportunity to end a conflict situation.

Dealing with a real life violent encounter will test you in ways that may be completely alien to your everyday life. Even if you have years of training experience, if attacked, you may not react in the way you think you will. Some martial arts like the ones described in this book develop skills that take years to perfect, but months to apply, and take you to a high level of skill and competency fast. They stem from an age where people fought hand to hand, discipline and punishment were severe and life was tough. Death was everywhere and the subject of fighting skill development was a serious undertaking.

For most in the world, life is now very different. We mostly live in peace but still have to deal with predatory individuals or groups that prey on others. To this end many people look to learn some form of self defence, usually a collection of techniques designed to be used in certain situations. The approach of some more recent systems is to teach in this way. Due to the fragmented nature of the syllabus taught, the student can often end up more confused than enlightened and when trying a technique against a more experienced adversary in reality, find to their cost that it does not have the desired effect.

Practical actions in self defence include any and all actions that will give you the physical and psychological edge. If it is to work for you in an encounter, you must take training seriously. Firstly, you must think the serious scenarios people have gone through and empathise. Listen to the daily news and you will probably hear a story of someone that has been viciously mugged, beaten, tortured, raped or murdered. When reflecting on this, even though you may not like to, the one fact to accept is, the people inflicting these horrors exist, and what they do, they do with no remorse, no pity and no feeling of right and wrong. Ignoring the fact may give you a greater sense of good in the world, but you inadvertently weaken yourself, when you cannot reason your way out of a situation, you have to physically face it.

The fact is, the world is made up of mainly good and well intentioned people, and techniques you learn may seem extreme in application, but it is sometimes necessary to take things to the extreme, you never know what or where your life may take you, and what situations you may find yourself in where these skills will unfortunately be required.

If a mugger pounces, they may shout and scream threats, maybe start the onslaught by physically punching or kicking you, maybe pull a knife, pistol or other weapon and demand what they want. They may be with a group and the attack may take you completely by surprise. Your home may be broken into, your shop, your business and you may be confronted by a very hostile individual or group. In all instances, how you react will be instinctive.

Someone highly trained will react without hesitation. The trained instinctive reaction will be to arm themselves and focus on and strike out at or neutralise the threat aggressively and then process the sensory overload from the bio-chemical reaction caused by the event, which becomes an attribute that powers your movements, making them swift and decisive. This kind of response becomes as instinctive as the untrained one of cowering or going into a ball when physically attacked.

Fear is a great motivator to aggression and heightened motor skills. Try to never develop an ego that erodes your sense of dread when in a serious situation, you will always stay sharp. The next time something completely unexpected makes you jump, take time to think about how you reacted to it. A car backfiring, someone behind you suddenly shouting loud acknowledgment to a friend across the street, a dog suddenly barking at you as you pass it by. If your reaction is to jump, gasp, hold your hands over your head while turning to look in the direction of the noise, you need to work on a better response. If you spin round in the direction of the sound, feel energy blast through your body with a sense of being drawn aggressively towards the source of the noise, you've been training a while. You may feel a little foolish afterwards either way, but if you respond in the second instance, as you turn to face an attacker, you will have the upper hand as you challenge them verbally and physically.

Verbal training creates assertiveness under stress. If someone is shouting at you, they are more likely to be focused on vocalisation to build up their confidence to attack you, if talking calmly to reason with them fails, vocalise your fear and shout back, this will empower you, and draw attention to your situation. Learning to shout and be heard is a technique used in many martial arts schools, it is also quite therapeutic. Learning to strike takes precedence.

Conditioning Mind and Body

We begin training by developing our hands. Hands are the primary striking tools. In order to use these tools effectively, conditioning the body is necessary. It is true that you can use all of the actions described in this book with no prior training, but the chances of sustaining injury increases significantly. If you must strike an adversary several times to deter them, it may not be possible if your hands are weak. You may have broken your wrist, knuckles or fingers with your first blow. In a situation like this, if you do manage to fight through, you will still have a long period of recuperation ahead of you while injuries heal.

Initially, you may find your wrists give way if you hit too hard. Injury is easy to sustain and takes months to recover from, which will put back your training schedule and progress, so take your time. After a workout, use a liniment, balm or rub on the areas worked on. Some Dit da Jow remedies work very well and aid in speedy recovery and the toughening process, these can be acquired from most good martial arts suppliers and schools. Over some time, your hands can become very hard at which point you can attempt focused striking practice. This can be on roof tiles, breeze blocks and wooden boards. Your hands are now able to withstand impact to solid targets.

In the beginning, slow and soft impact conditioning on a wall bag, punch bag or strawboard are recommended. The idea is to build up the strength of your bones, muscle and skin tissue in order to use that area to impact force into an object. The harder the object, the better your conditioning needs to be. With a wall bag, initially it is best to fill it with rice. As your wrists strengthen and the bones in your hands become stronger, you can fill the bag with dry peas, then as the bones and joints become even stronger and the skin more calloused and thick, you can fill it with steel BB's or sand. When starting out, a period of six months of daily wall bag training should be done before moving onto a harder filling. Practice striking with fists, palm heels, finger tips and hand edges. Work the striking power slowly into the bag; get to know your weaknesses by repetitive striking using just enough force. Over time you will be able to put your entire body weight behind each strike.

Conditioning hurts, and takes determination. When your knuckles are bruised and bleeding we fight through it, when skin is ripped off on the wall bag and your fists are torn up, you must keep going back to it. Day after day, you are getting used to the pain of the exercise and the sting of the Jow, this develops your body your mind.

Breathing

Whenever you are training, keep breathing deep, full and steady. Actions should be performed with speed, power and flow. You should be able to train at a good pace for two hours without fatigue. The slower and deeper the breath, the less calories are being converted over a longer period of time so you have sustained levels of energy which you use efficiently. In short, you fight for longer at maximum power.

Mind, Energy/Yi, Chi

Western science and medicine defines Chi as bio-electricity, which pulses through our nervous system, stimulating muscles which make our body and limbs perform actions. The mind/Yi leads the Energy/Chi into performing the actions of the body.

Stand with your feet shoulder width apart. Relax yourself by taking a deep breath and slowly let it out. As you do, feel the weight over your feet increase as your body relaxes and you sink further into the floor. Close your eyes and concentrate on breathing very slowly, in then out. Relax all the joints of the body while maintaining the upright standing position. Feel the belly expand and contract as you breathe in and out through the nose. Repeat ten times and with each exhale try to relax your body more and more until your feet feel firmly pressed and rooted to the spot.

Repeat the exercise as often as you need to until you can reach the relaxed state at will. Just try it now, think about your shoulders and back, are they tense? If they are, take a deep breathe and allow yourself to relax as you breathe out, become aware of your tension. If you have trouble getting to sleep, focus on the sound of your breathe and again allow your body to relax, do not be distracted. Slow, deep breathes will get you to sleep.

When you can relax at will, face a wall and standing a foot from it, place your palms on the wall. Keep your elbows by your sides and press the wall through an upward angle. Slowly increase the force you press into the wall until you can feel your feet being pressed into the floor. As you hold this position, concentrate on the feeling of the energy moving through your body from hands to feet, become aware of the energy. Now try and repeat the feeling but without using the wall, imagine it is there and resisting you. Apply this awareness of energy to any action you practice.

Understanding Chi flow leads to energy concepts in martial application. Inch Force/Chuen Ging and Explosive Force/Fa Ging are a few of the many expressions of energy used in fighting and are slowly developed in practice. The most famous example being Bruce Lees inch punch. To develop it properly takes time and persistence.

Re-Training Instinctive Behaviour

If you study someone that has no fighting experience, you will notice that for the most part, when struck at, their instinct is to move the hands up in front of their head and face. This reaction is due to the fact that we are instinctively aware that the brain, eyes, ears, jaw and nose must be protected from damage for us to effectively breathe, see, hear and nourish ourselves.

Trained reaction on the other hand, teaches you to throw your arms forward and up, meeting the line of force, at which point you have bridged with, decelerated or deflected the incoming force away and momentarily dissolved the threat. We take preservation of our faculties very seriously, nothing gets through.

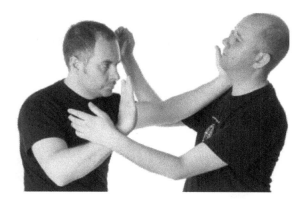

The range at which fighting takes place will vary depending on experience. A fight between two people that are Un-trained will usually start at long range, then after several attempts to strike, will move into the grappling range or the clinch. This is again instinctively what happens as the mind and body are aware that flailing arms and legs can do more damage when freely thrown around. We want total control over the opponent with an ability to strike at will.

The Hand Weapons

Shapes we create and apply with our limbs move in a way that creates weight or mass to that part of our body. The fist is thrown and hits the target, with a hardened hand. If that hand is left relaxed until the very end of the movement, and suddenly tightens into a fist, the hand hits with a whipping or snapping action. The solid object of the hand, hits very hard, but the line of energy it has been powered through continues to move through the opponent. The energy of the impact causes bruising, internal bleeding, and in extreme cases, organ failure.

This shock force can also smash solid objects, which when applied in fighting, are the skull and bones of our opponent. The skull and bones in themselves, when struck and broken, send many fragments of bone, into the soft, internal organs, muscle and cartilage of the body. This causes pain, injury and damage that can immobilise or even kill an adversary.

Straight Thrusting Punch/Jic Chung Choi

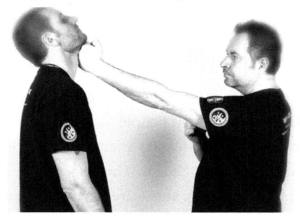

The thrusting punch begins with the fist on your centre line, approximately a fist distance forward from your solar plexus. From here, if the path is clear, it is thrust forward in a straight line to the centre of the opponent. As the fist is thrust forward its path rises with the rising of your elbow. In application, the fist continues on a straight line path, connects with the opponents centre, lifting them out of their stance. If the opponent starts with their fist in this position, bring your wrist onto the centre instead of the fist. As your opponent thrusts their fist forward, you do the same, and as the structures meet, your wrist will deflect their punching arm, while your fist continues on to the target.

From its start position, your fist and forearm presents an obstacle to the opponent if they are attempting to control you by pressing your chest. By simply connecting to the inside or outside of their wrist and pressing your fist forwards, you take control of their pressing force. If they let go and attempt to strike you, you thrust your fist at them. You should only concern yourself with thrusting the hand forwards and at the target. Try to avoid tensing the arm before and during the strike, this will slow it down and will cause you to use sideward, resisting force should the punch be bridged.

If your punch is deflected or blocked to the side, follow up with another punch from your other arm, continue throwing them out until you hit the opponent or force them to retreat or bridge your arms.

Ginger Fist/Gurn Choi

This fist is formed by bending all the fingers tightly and then pressing the thumb tip into the side of the index finger, then squeezing the little finger against the other bent fingers. The pressure from the thumb and the little finger compress all the fingers together forming a very hard tool. You can strike with the knuckle tips, main knuckles or inside of the hand. Primarily though, it is striking with the tips of the knuckles to the throat or ribs, nerves on the arms and legs.

Phoenix Eye Fist/Fung Nan Choi

This hand structure is formed by making a fist and then pressing the thumb against the nail of the index finger. This then projects the first phalange of the index finger forwards which is then supported by the thumb. Striking force is concentrated at the point of the first phalange. It is an extremely effective tool as its striking power is thrust into a very small and localised area, it can do severe damage to the nerves in the face, body arm and legs, by striking pressure points and muscles. It can also be pressed into these areas to effect an electric shock type reaction from an opponent which can be useful in taking their balance or moving them out of your path.

Chopping Arm/Fak Sao

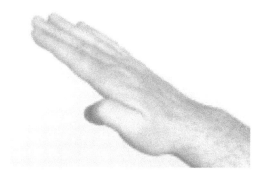

When square facing the opponent, drive the hand edge forward. For more power, use the waist to lead the chopping action and smash the edge of the hand, wrist or forearm into the target. Attack the ribs, neck or side of head for maximum results.

Closing Fist/Sao Kuen

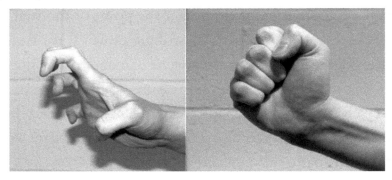

Train to strengthen the fingers in the closing action and they can be used as a weapon. Tense the fingers and hold them in a bent position to use them in a clawing motion attacking the eyes, throat and hair. When closing the fist, start with the little finger first, this will improve grip. When the fist is closed, train to hold it as tightly as you can, this will increase wrist and forearm power.

The Leg Weapons

When training thrusting kicking dynamics, learn to twist the hip forward to extend the kick further. The twist should occur as the heel of the foot reaches and hits its target. Once you have this ability and can kick with full power while remaining balanced, train with a step moving you into the kick to increase its power. Commit the heel to the straight line swinging upward and it will hit the opponent at any point between their incoming ankle and their incoming hip. Always throw it out with maximum force while remaining balanced.

If you can do this kick effectively, you should then train to combine a punch with the kick.

The lead leg kick is fast, and attacks any point from the opponents ankle to the pelvis. The ideal targets are the knee and groin as these areas are weaker and if hit correctly, can drop an opponent immediately.

The rear leg kick is more powerful but a lot slower and more easily seen by the opponent. Best used when you have contact with the opponents arms.

In footwork, we learn to attack with a punch, a kick or both together. We learn to blast forward and backward, stay coiled ready to pounce. We learn to throw the energy from the moving stance, through the waist, elbow, wrist and fist. Punch and kick like you mean it, but learn range so you can place the punch within a millimetre of your training partner's body with full power thrown from that point, your partner will feel the wind hit them. In application, punch and kick through the opponent.

If a kick is thrown at you, stay out of range or step forward and intercept it. You will take its power before it reaches full momentum. Step back and its full force will hit you.

Ascending Heel/Dang Gurk

We use this action to intercept the opponents centre or kicking leg. We stop a kick, with a kick. Simply lift your foot higher then the incoming upward kick, and let it kick the sole of your shoe. If the opponents kick is not committed you will kick them, applying this at the correct range is important.

Wing Leg/Bong Gerk

This can be applied as a kicking action or a deflection, as seen in the wooden man form. Applying the deflection, as the opponents kick comes in, meet it with your lower leg by rotating your foot to the side and throwing the knee up and out in an arc. After bridging the incoming leg, follow on by moving forward to attack or follow their heel back to the floor, apply Huen Ma/Pak Da and trip them.

If the kick is travelling high, intercept with Gahn Jam Sao or Kwun Sao and Chai Gurk.

Stamp Kick/Chai Gurk

Applied to the knee, shin, foot and anywhere on the body if used when trampling on an opponent that has fallen.

Stand square on and then thrust your heel forward and to your centre. The heel should go out no higher than your waist. This technique can be used as a follow up to the Dang Gurk, if the opponent has stepped back to avoid the first kick. When applied, as in the other kicking techniques, the heel of the kicking foot should be in line with the knee of the supporting leg, in order to protect it from the opponents counter kick. When this kick makes contact with the intended target, drive your bodyweight down through it, either breaking the opponents leg or forcing them to fall.

Turning Front Kick with Heel/Wang Gurk

Aim at extending the kick through the pelvis, smashing the pelvic girdle back, which thrusts the lower back out, folding the opponent and destroying their balance. Try to time the kick with the opponent moving in at you.

When combined with a kick, the punch, the kick, or both may find the target. If the punch is bridged, the kick should find its target. If the arms become bridged, your initial strike will fail to hit effectively but may have inadvertently also intercepted and dissipated an incoming punch from your opponent.

Your opponent may have stopped your first strike, but when they stick with your arm after the initial interception, they give you an insight into where their energy and intention is going. This "Bridge" effectively turns your punching arm into a feeling arm, and where it feels resistance, it finds an opening. At this stage of practice you will feel this in a millisecond, being able to control their balance, weapons and centre.

This concept is in theory very easy to understand, but takes years to master to the point where you react without thought, when you can feel your opponents force is not threatening, or focused at your centre, you flow around their physical structures and find their centre. The basic point is this, whenever your opponent moves their intention up, down, right, left, you can take their centre, because you only focus your intent at their centre. This is a frustrating concept in the beginning of your training, but highly rewarding when understood. There are no shortcuts to obtaining the skill of feeling, you must train daily and for prolonged periods.

Train to kick without moving your upper body or giving any signal of intent through your arms. Extend training to look at sweeping, pressing with the knee, stomping and scraping.

When arms are in contact, pull your partners arms violently downwards when feeling the shift in their body structure as they attempt to kick. This will return their lifting foot to the floor and give you the opportunity to strike them.

If you face an aggressor with good kicking techniques, use the iron bridge to smash the feet, ankles and legs and rush the centre.

Attacking the weak areas

Some people are naturally more resilient to others when hit, they can absorb much more punishment, and fight through even when injured. They may be strongly built, highly athletic, have great stamina and high tolerance to pain. When applying Wing Chun in reality, when defending your life, you attack and hit vital targets until your opponent is down. The following are universally understood to be the hardest areas to condition and so remain vulnerable when attacked.

The groin

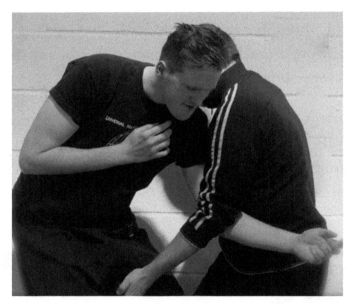

When grabbing the testicles, like a dog with a new toy, squeeze, twist and rag it as hard and fast as you can, ignore the screaming, only stopping when you can move safely to the next target. Strike that area with any and every technique, as often as you can during the fight, that and the throat.

The throat

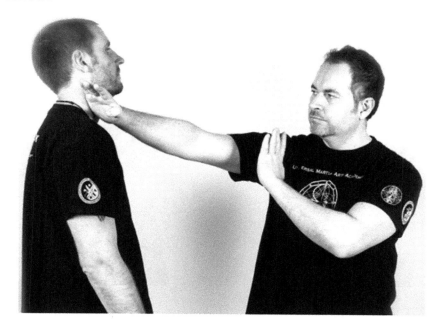

Chopping or punching the throat lightly can create a gag reflex, harder can crush the windpipe. The windpipe is very delicate in striking terms, it can be crushed, squeezed and torn easily. The closing fist/Sao Kuen action that features at the end of most actions in form teaches the fist to be closed through rolling fingers, pinky to index through to the thumb. If your thumb and fingers are thrust either side of the windpipe, deep into the throat, it is at this point we close the fingers tightly around it, the effect is serious.

The eyes

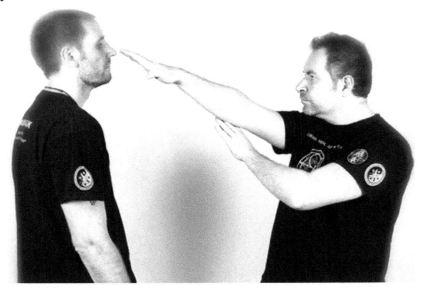

Most attackers will expect to see who they are attacking. A well placed flick of a knuckle, finger or thumb in their eye causes the head to reflex back and away from the object hitting it, this is an instinct that is hard to ignore. The eyes water, vision blurs and there is extreme discomfort, making it difficult for the attacker to concentrate on you. If the situation is more dire, drive the fingers or thumbs hard into the eyes. Move from the eyes to groin to throat in fast succession, if one hits, all the others can follow.

The ears

Cupping or slapping the ears can devastate a persons balance and co-ordination and cause long term damage. Actions from forms introducing this action should be examined and the movement applied efficiently. Throw the slap with the power of a hooking punch, knock them off their feet as you deafen them. Harder still and you also damage their neck and spine.

The Hands

If the opponent hangs their fists in front of you, punch them, or drive knuckles into the back of their fists, this breaks the small bones easily. Whenever hands are in range, smash them.

Fingers

Whenever you get the chance in a fight, grab, squeeze, rotate and break fingers. If you manage to get a firm grip, don't let go, even after you have broken them, twisting and ragging the fingers further until the opponent is down. This will tear tendons and muscle in the forearms and takes a very long time to recover from, worth doing if an attacker has a weapon, they can never use again.

The elbow

A fully committed strike will usually be thrown with the arm becoming fully extended at the elbow. Learn to guide their arm past you while getting your body either under or over it and smash or roll it into a lock or break.

Look to hyper-extend your opponents arm and attack the elbow with leverage applied from your waist rotation, body weight and energy projected from your elbows.

The knee

If the opponent stands straight and you see their lead leg locked out, stomp your heel down onto the knee, you will either break the leg or drop the opponent.

The foot

Stamp on the attackers instep at the same time as going for the eyes or throat. The bones of the foot, like the hand, are very weak in comparison to other areas. Every time you step, look to stamp your heel down hard onto the metatarsal bones in order to break the opponent's foot. If the opponent is heavy set, they will have trouble putting their bodyweight back on that foot, and so their striking force becomes limited. If their foot is broken, attack it again, or drive your heel into their shin, causing them more problems.

Spending time training to attack the weak areas reinforces their vulnerability in your mind, and this awareness prevents you from making mistakes that expose your weak areas in combat.

Basic Martial Arts Theory

If you are naturally assertive and aggressive you can learn to be softer and calmer, if you are overly passive, you can learn to be more assertive and physically capable, whatever your personality when you come to practice, it offers you balance.

Martial arts training primarily involves learning to use shapes to create deflecting structures and striking tools to deal with an opponent. These can take the form of the square (basic destructive shape), triangular (piercing aggressive shape) and the circular (advanced flowing shape). Each shape in moving application can cancel out the other. This should be trained and understood.

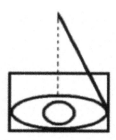  

The square method deals with aggressive lines of force by using the arms to block an adversary's strike and bounce it off to the sides, up or down and away from the our head and body. This should be combined with a counter attack that strikes back at the opponent along a straight line. This method is highly effective if the opponent is tense; i.e. punching with a tightly clenched fist; as the deflecting block can smash against the tense arm or leg with a sideward action, causing severe damage to the opponent's limbs.

The triangular method deals with an opponent's incoming force by deflecting strikes away from our centre and off to the sides of the body. It is achieved by driving a triangle, pyramid or wedge shape angle formed usually from the wrist to the elbow, forward and into the path of the incoming attacking limbs. When done correctly the adversary is lead to think that they are still attacking in a straight line because their strike is still moving forwards, albeit into empty space. The triangular method deflects the incoming strike away from the defenders centre and just past the outer gate or silhouette of the torso and head. As it does so, it leaves the opponents head or body on a crash course with our counter strike; which has now taken the centre line.

This method is very effective for those that are smaller and weaker than their opponent, as the entire body is behind the technique, little effort is required to utilise the principles. In order to achieve the correct result, the practitioner must develop a sense of grounding and an ability to drive their structural power from the feet, through the body and into the opponent.

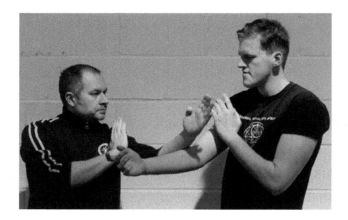

The circular spherical method is used to intercept, absorb and move in time with the opponent's incoming force. At high levels of understanding, the opponent can literally be moved around while they commit to a line of attack. This is considered one of the highest levels of skill.

You simply wait for the aggressor to start moving, allow them to build up momentum, then aggressively connect to their incoming limb while simultaneously moving yourself out of its flight path.

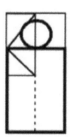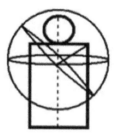

If the attack is strong, chances are the opponent is so intent on reaching you, that they lose their balance, their mass increases, you get out of the way, and they throw themselves into a wall or other object. It teaches us to absorb, parry and deflect aggressive force whilst allowing us to remain balanced, upright and capable of echoing the attackers power thrown at us, sending it straight back through them.

Although all methods can be utilised in this manner, to cause the effect just described, the circular and triangular methods are the most subtle ways of dealing with an opponent. They can lead them almost effortlessly into a lock, throw or strike.

The sphere can be small or large, contracted or expanded to meet the opponent's physical position. The sphere can remain or it can collapse into the triangle, wedge, pyramid or box. Combining the sphere with the triangle creates the teardrop, which manifests itself as slingshot force, borrowed from, and thrown back at the opponent.

Ranges of Physical Combat and the Defensive Sphere

A complete system of combat utilises all fighting ranges, including adding weaponry to extend the effective range. Empty hand skills will start at long range using the legs to attack. At full extension this would be a front, horizontal kick using the ball of the foot, the heel kick, the finger jab, ginger fist, the thumb and fist. Next is the palm or wrist, knee, elbow, shoulder, hip and head butt. If you start fighting at body checking range, the tools used are then applied in reverse order. Fighting strategy uses kicks at long range, hands at medium range, elbows and grappling at close range. Turning the torso and waist extends these ranges further as does moving and stepping in at the opponent.

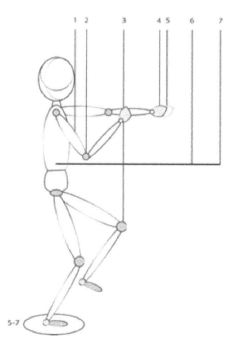

1. Body Checking Range
2. Fixed Elbow Defensive Range
3. Elbow/Knee Range
4. Punch/Palm Range
5. Finger Range
6. Rotated Waist Extended Striking Range
7. Extended Kicking Range

Recognising when your personal space is encroached is developed in training. The first form in the Wing Chun system teaches you to think of mental way-points that become an imaginary sphere that you exist within. We do it instinctively before practicing form in a crowded class to make sure we don't accidentally hit our classmates.

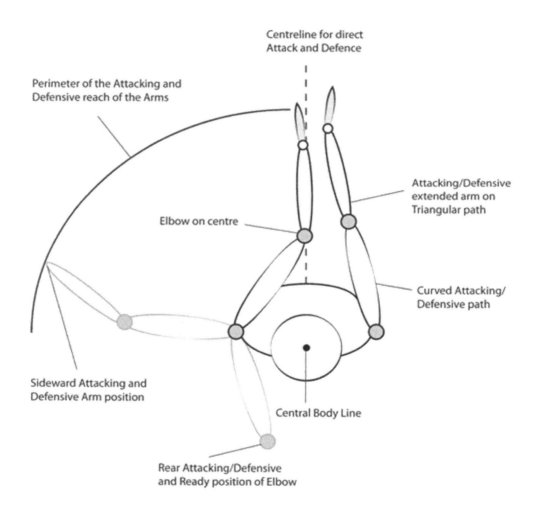

Centreline for direct
Attack and Defence

Perimeter of the Attacking and
Defensive reach of the Arms

Attacking/Defensive
extended arm on
Triangular path

Elbow on centre

Curved Attacking/
Defensive path

Sideward Attacking and
Defensive Arm position

Central Body Line

Rear Attacking/Defensive
and Ready position of Elbow

As an exercise, stretch your arms as fully as you can in front of you and place your palms together, then stretch your fingers as far as you can and hold them firmly forward. Now draw a half circle by stretching your arms out to your sides. This is half the perimeter of the defensive, fighting sphere. The defensive fighting shapes you make with your arms can travel anywhere in this sphere and deal with any position or technique.

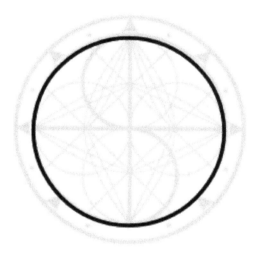

From arms outstretched to the sides, bring them around to the front of your chest, and press your palms together. If you now look at the point where your palms meet, you will see, formed from your shoulders along your arms and to your hands, the structure of the triangle. The movement made to bring your arms to the front of your body was made through a reversed half circle. This is the basic idea of forming and moving through the shapes and structures of the circle, or semi circle, and the triangle.

Now put your hands at your sides. Pulling your elbows together your wrists will align in front of your chin. You draw a half circle with your elbows that terminates at the point of the triangle pointing out from your centre, the upper arm bones providing the structure to this shape. This is the forming and moving through the, inner circle and triangle that you defend with your elbows, covering the ribs and solar plexus.

The weight of your arm structures come from the inner half circle. To understand this do the same exercise as above, but this time the point of focus is in the elbows, which are brought to the sides with powerful torque. Once understood, you can move power to the wrists when needed in striking, and in the elbows when redirecting force. Therefore the wrists draw a large half circle and the elbows the small half circle. This requires a reasonable amount of flexibility to achieve.

This flexibility is one aspect that is slowly developed when practicing the first form in the systems syllabus. A good way to attain it is to hold a tennis ball between the elbows for 5-10 minutes, this will give you the stretch and feel for the positions the elbows must move through when practicing.

The outer triangle is excellent for deflecting a strike at long range, wrist to wrist. It can be driven in as a wedge that deflects the opponent's attack away from you while keeping your hands aimed at their centre and then brings you to the close range position. The inner triangle is better suited to dealing with structures that are already at close range, using body weight and torque from waist rotation, the fixed elbow creates strong leverage against the opponent's wrist.

When contact is made with the opponent's arm, if it continues to press at you, you stay with it. If their force presses anywhere but at you, you can remove it or let it go, either by disconnecting from their arm or by flowing into another snaking structure. This will free up your arm and let their arm travel on the path of its owner's intent, away from your body, leaving you free to strike.

When you can meet incoming force with control, and stick to it while allowing it to 'root' you to the spot, you create a strong yet flexible barrier between you and your opponent. The feeling is manifested in the hands, which physically enforce or create the feeling of a defensive perimeter around you. When using this skill, your energy can be passive, lightly controlling and yielding or strong, forceful and aggressive.

Holding your open hands up in front of you creates a subtle battle ready position, it may seem totally passive to the enemy, but we are holding them up ready to deflect or sink arms that come at us and strike the opponent when they move into range.

Palms also look less offensive if witnessed by onlookers, but can be delivered with devastating power.

If the punch is thrown at your face, drive your punch from underneath the opponents arm, as your elbow rises, you will hit and bounce theirs up and away from you while your punch will land. The attacking hand is also the defensive hand.

Whatever angle you use to deflect an attacking arm or leg, the idea is to counter attack as quickly as possible.

Don't train the arms to just deflect strikes away, attack the opponent's arms when their body or head cannot be seen. Every strike is a block and every block is a strike.

Concepts within Sui Lum Tao

The Mountain Stance/Yee Jee Kim Yuen Ma

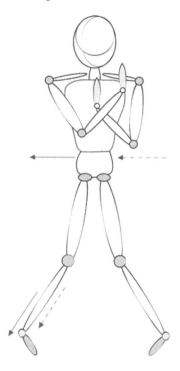

Watching most professional fighters, in any form, if they are evenly matched they inevitably always reach a point where they clinch, unless the fight is ended quickly through a knock out or submission. The clinch normally comes about because one fighter becomes fatigued and needs to rest, or needs to bring the opponents arms under control because they are too fast. When the clinch comes about, the fighter skilled in feeling intention through contact reflex and sensitivity to energy, has the upper hand. The deeper level of understanding, gaining a perception and awareness of an opponent's energy and intent is learned through 'feeling'.

To begin training the skill of 'feeling' we must first understand stance. A good fighting stance should be well balanced, strong and stable, yet flexible. You should be able to move powerfully backwards, forwards and sideways from a neutral stance. To achieve this without signalling your intention, your legs should be relaxed in application, with your body weight suspended by the knees, and an awareness of that weight pressing the feet into the floor.

It is important to concentrate on feeling your bodies balance spread over the soles of your feet. Weight should be held over the middle of the feet so if you are pressed, you may allow a shift of body weight over the heels, and if pulled, allow a shift of body weight over the toes.

In both cases, these slight movements indicate the possible need to shift into a forward fighting stance or allow a rotation of the waist to deflect the pressing force. Whether you move one leg forward or backward when pressed or pulled, you are moving into a forward fighting stance.

The better your feeling for being in a balanced square on stance, the more difficult it is for someone to move you. When external forces are applied to your body, we do not resist by moving against it the directed pressure, instead we increase the energy within our body structure. This is the first principle of force redirection, accepting incoming force and allowing it to move through you and into the ground.

When in the mountain stance, relax your legs and feel the energy in the knees and waist, which feel like a coiled spring. Bend the knees until they are in line with your toes, tilt your hips forward and hold energy in the pelvis. The energy in the waist extends up the spine to the neck and is held in alignment. When in the stance you should meditate to feel the energy from the feet to the neck. When this is understood and trained, it will become instinctive and will exist without conscious thought, you will instinctively have a strong and balanced body structure.

When understood, it is possible to take pressure pushing the body and redirect it into the ground from literally any angle by making tiny adjustments in position relative to the energy moving through. The aim is to find the optimum position in your balance so you will be ready to absorb prying or pressing force even when not strictly in the stance. Performing its actions over some years will give you the ability to perform its intended purpose from practically any position, whether on one leg or both. This can only be achieved when you can feel and route the pressing force that is applied to you, which is guided to the ground by minute changes in the angle of the arms, torso and legs.

When starting the form, stand with your feet together and get a sense of your balance and weight sinking into the spot you are stood on. Take a deep breath and as you let it out, pull your arms back, fists clenched tightly and held one inch from the sides of your chest. While you pull the hands back, simultaneously sink your body weight further into your stance by bending your knees so they line up with the front of you toes.

Now briefly leaning weight on your heels, create a 'V' by turning your toes outwards. Then place your bodyweight over the balls of your feet and turn your heels outward. From here, your feet are pointing in and form an imaginary triangle, pointing out from your toes to the tip of the triangle, which is where your opponent's centre will be. Angle your pelvis up slightly and relax your bodyweight into the stance, holding it all together with a slight muscular tension in the thighs and butt. Keep your back straight, chin up and chest held slightly forwards. There is buoyancy in this stance that exists at the knees. If weight or pressure is placed on the hips, the knees and feet can absorb this force until the feeling of pressing out from the floor exists.

If we are pressed by the opponent, our body structure and stance can absorb the pressing force while we remain balanced and rooted to the floor. When pressed with greater force, we rotate and deflect the force away from our centre.

The same principle applies if slowly and gradually pressed back. If the pressure on your chest is gradually built up and then suddenly disconnects, your legs will spring you out from the floor and in the direction of the pressing force, one leg will move forward and you will arrive in a strong, forward stance.

Once in the stance you should maintain your balance and posture. When training with a partner, never allow yourself to overextend your arms or you will give away your balance. If during exercises you are pulled or pushed, try to maintain your position.

A good way to develop further power from the stance is to stand with a 3-5kg medicine ball held pressed between the knees, if you can support it there for 10 minutes you will have developed a strong stance.

When in class, or for the duration of your allotted practice time, remain in the stance. This is the first stage of leg development for powerful stepping, kicking, sweeping and deflecting. Align energy, feel it move into the ankles, knees, waist and elbows. The lower spine and neck are connected by this energy, which keeps the spine straight, learn to stretch the spine as the energy moves up to the neck and hold the stretch, this is training. The torso is aligned with the angle of the thigh, which gives the appearance of the torso tilting back.

Ha Cha Sao/Seung Cha Sao

Crossing the arms defines the centre line. Do this in your mind prior to entering into the stance.

This action involves crossing the arms at the wrist, first in a downward motion, then fixing the elbows and bringing the hands up and rotating the palms to face you. Where the hands cross should lie exactly on your centre. The hands pointing down define the left and right lower gates or zones, and when pointing up, define the left and right middle gates. When an attacking limb enters each zone, the corresponding defensive technique is applied to that zone.

On the second action, as you rotate the hands and lift them, they draw an imaginary line up your centre. This action also defines the Gahn Sao and Tan Sao actions, used later with the Yui Ma.

To take this further than simply moving the hands down, up and back, resistance can be held between the wrists for torso development. The left wrist pressing down on the right, which resists upwards from the low position, and the left wrist pushing out against the right wrist pulling in the upper position. As you disconnect the wrists this resistance, gives a hint of 'Fa Ging' as you elbows spring backward.

In form, when holding the elbows back, pull the elbows in toward your spine, to stretch the back and shoulders. Also, rotate the wrist and fist so the knuckle of your little finger is higher than your index finger and close the fist tightly. This will stretch and strengthen your forearms and grip. Keep the fists an inch from your sides. The body should now begin to feel strong and stretched. In transition, the fist stays relaxed until impact.

The Straight Thrusting Punch/Jic Chung Choi

The straight thrusting punch should be learned in stages. From a relaxed shoulder learn to swing the elbow from your side towards the tip of the inside triangle. Once this can be performed quickly and effortlessly, feel the elbow drive the wrist and fist towards the target. Feel the energy from the elbow transfer through the forearm and manifest in the fist, which clenches on impact.

Once you have this fully understood begin to train to feel the feet in stance and body structure support the elbow and fist when driven into a punchbag. The punch should be thrown with the feeling of firing an arrow from a bow, relaxed and effortless. No power is held in the shoulder. Train to let the energy in the forearm relax back into the elbow and knees after the punch is thrown.

The elbow is always angled down at the floor, only ever extend the arm fully when connecting and driving the fist through the target. Whether your elbow is over or under the opponents arm, you can use it to control or deflect their striking action. By combining these actions we begin to learn the concept of linked attack and defence/Lin Sui Dai Da.

Pulling Hand/Lap Sao.

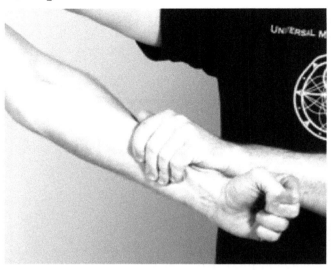

This pulling or jerking action is very effective at bringing an adversary closer for better control, as well as helping you regain your balance if shoved, or dragging the opponent past you. As an opposing action you can use the Lap Sao along with pressing force/Bik Ging with your other arm or torso to place stress on or break limbs. If successfully applied, Lap Sao is quick and can cause whiplash or even break the neck of the opponent.

The action that the hand performs, 'grabbing' and 'pulling', exists only for a second. Lap Sao can be applied anywhere on the body and is highly effective when used on arms, the head and hair, the jaw and fingers. It can also be used to disarm an aggressor by pulling the weapon quickly from their hands.

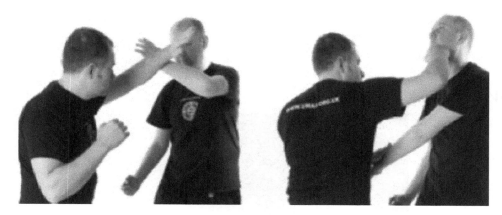

If used effectively and efficiently, the Lap Sao should be guided by the direction of opponent's attacking energy. You must have a contact with their arm and as you feel your arm being pressed, pull their wrist and accelerate their arm off centre. If done correctly, this will lead the opponent effortlessly into a throw, lock or strike.

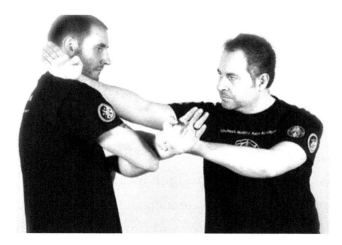

To counter the Lap Sao, try applying Circling/Huen Sao to slide free of the grip as it goes on, or move forward with the pulling action and crash their centre with your shoulder or head. It is important that you do not get used to poor posture by allowing a training partner to constantly compromise your position when using a strong Lap Sao action. In the initial stage of training, applying and receiving the Lap Sao action should be done while balanced, stationary and square on to each other.

Withdrawn Elbow/Chun Jarn

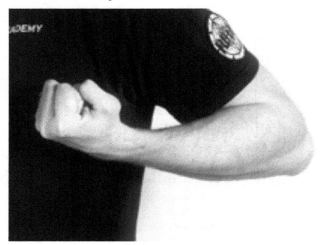

This withdrawing elbow can be used to smash into an opponent at your side. It also teaches correct application of withdrawing opposing energy while keeping the arm relaxed and the body balanced. All of the elbow movements strike with immense power.

In form the elbow should be held, stretched back with a slight tension through the fist, which is kept an inch away from the side of the body. The elbow is pulled back to create a stretch around the chest, shoulder and back. This teaches good form and posture and the ability to fix one arms position while the other one moves, essential to future training concepts of moving around an opponent using the 'fixed' elbow, it also promotes flexibility and concentration.

Spreading Hand/Tan Sao

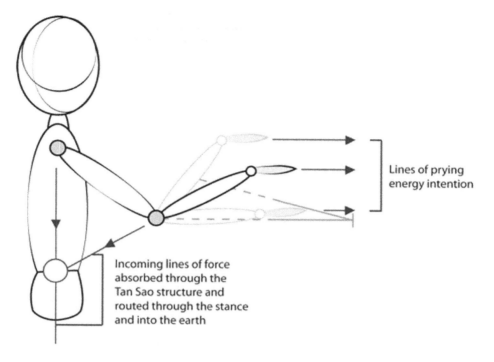

Lines of prying energy intention

Incoming lines of force absorbed through the Tan Sao structure and routed through the stance and into the earth

This palm up, prying and spreading position can connect to the inside and outside of the opponent's arms or legs. On the inside of the opponent's arm, it should be held towards and past the opponent's shoulder. On the outside of the opponent's arm this can be held at the opponent's centre.

From the inside, the opponent's arm is over the top of the Tan Sao position. If they disconnect from your arm, you can hit them in the face, if they fight the structure before they disconnect, borrow any downward force they may give you and feel your elbow coil into your stance, ready to strike them if they let your arm fly free or come around their arm to strike.

From the outside, the Tan Sao is on top of their arm, energy from their arm pressing into your elbow, here you should focus your energy down at the opponent's chest or abdomen, any counter resistance will press up, at which point, if your arm is freed, you will hit down to the solar plexus area, forward to the chest or up towards the face, again depending on where the opponent's force was pressing.

Tan Sao is strong at the elbow and weak at the wrist. In form, its practice begins to develop the idea of the arm being like a bamboo cane, strong yet flexible.

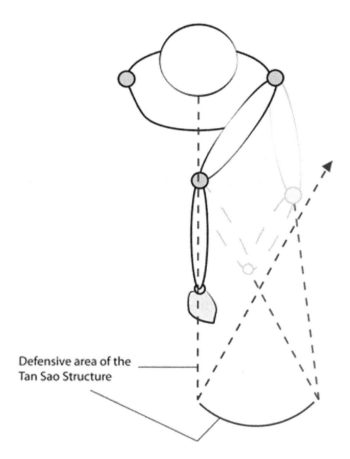

Defensive area of the
Tan Sao Structure

Open space is created between you and the opponent by connecting this shape to the opponent's arm and then rotating the torso while keeping the elbow of the structure fixed at your centre. It can be applied with outward or downward rotation to throw off an attack, can be connected to an attacking arm and forced back and to the side, thrust forward into the path of a straight or circling line of force or lifted up through the centre to connect to and throw an incoming line of force up into the air.

The Tan Sao can be applied with wrenching force to split an opponent's arms or defensive position apart and aggressively open them up to attacks to the inside or outside of the body and head. The rotation of the wrist is also of relevance as it can create an extra inch of diverting structural space for you to work with and take the opponent's force just off your centre line. Your wrist being wider horizontally across. Its power lies in the elbow, which is supported by the stance and hips. If downward pressure is applied onto the elbow, the Tan Sao can stay, and is stronger than the downward force, and you can uproot the opponent.

If this same pressure is applied to the wrist, we use the next action in the sequence to come around the pressure and retake the centre-line.

Circling Hand/Huen Sao

The circling action of the hand takes place with a small rotation at the elbow and the larger rotation at the wrist. This action is usually practiced with the hands energy dispersing to the side, moving the palm to the inside or outside of the opponent's arm, in this way though, the energy, although temporarily, is being focused in the wrong direction. Focusing it to the sides is inefficient. In form, press your wrist downward slightly while keeping it on centre as you rotate the hand, first so your palm heel lines up with the side of the imaginary opponent's torso, then, as the hand comes up into the Man Sao structure allow your elbow to move out slightly so it lines up with the side of your torso or outside gate/Oi Mun.

Energy in the actions moves from the elbow to wrist and back again like water. Imagine your forearm is half full of water, as you drop your wrist lower than your elbow the water fill the hand, making it heavy, the reverse then makes the elbow heavier. Huen Sao is one action where this analogy is important to understand.

When applying the Huen Sao, you must get a good contact at the wrist and press that contact forward and down, the hand then rotates forwards also, moving inside the opponent's arm if they stay and then striking them, or coming back round and swallowing the opponent's arm if it moves forward to attack. If your arm is inside their arm, you can move through the Huen Sao to arrive on the outside of their arm, in either Pak or Man Sao.

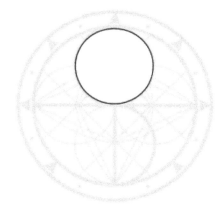

By pressing the wrist of the Huen Sao action down slightly, your force is moving against the opponent's forward force as opposed to pressing energy off to the sides and into thin air. This will cause the opponent to come around your structure which is still on centre, making them move inefficiently. If the opponent disconnects at any point during the execution of this movement your hand is free to strike.

Asking Hand/Man Sao

The arm is held out, elbow pointing to the ground, hand in the praying palm position. The arm is not fully extended so it cannot easily be locked or controlled at the elbow. If a strike is thrown at you and makes contact with the outside of the Man Sao structure, the angle of the elbow is held firm with forward pressing force which will divert any forwarding strike away from the body.

The Man Sao position tracks the opponent's movement when no contact exists between you. Man Sao must be constantly focused on your opponent's centre with forwarding energy. When they move to your right, you track them with your right hand, if they then cross over to your left side, just as they pass your centre-line, you switch positions so your left arm becomes the extended Man Sao, and your right hand is pulled back to become the rear guard hand position (Wu Sao). At this stage again though, just focus it out from your centre.

It is important to mention that when outstretching your hands and using a "guard," a skilled opponent may attempt to strike or slash at them, so you should be ready to move your hands out of the way. A safe way to do this is to retract your lead hand while simultaneously thrusting out your rear guard hand, the two hands simply changing positions while the opponent's attempted attack passes them by. As your skill progresses you can use these opportunities to strike the opponent as they are focused on chasing your moving hand and not on what your other hand is doing. As your skill progresses further, you can have the intention of Man Sao existing between you and the opponent without the physical structure actually being there until the opponent moves in at you.

In application, the Man Sao does not chase the opponent's arm to make contact, instead, it allows the opponent's attacking limb to make contact with it, if the opponent's attack then forces its way down the arm and at your centre, by feeling the direction of their attacking energy, you can thrust the structure forwards, simultaneously striking them with the hand and causing a deflection at the angled elbow of the Man Sao structure. You can also change the Man Sao into another deflecting structure to redirect the attack away from your centre. If their attacking limb makes contact and then seeks a new way around to you, the Man Sao immediately changes into a thrusting strike at the opponent's incoming head.

In defence, using Man Sao we think of a 3 sided force, over the wrist, in the palm and from the hand edge. This exists through Jum Sao and Wu Sao.

Sinking Hand/Jum Sao

From the Man Sao, you draw your elbow position back, following the angle your forearm is angled at, sinking the elbow down towards your hips while keeping the palm or hand edge on centre, the withdrawing hand stops and is held a fist distance form your chest. It is important that your intent and energy are focused at the elbow and wrist, as these are primarily what are controlling the partners attempted attack.

This sinking elbow action can also start with the arm extended out from the shoulder and the elbow outside and off the centre. As the opponent's arm enters and moves towards your centre, you draw your elbow across and back into your centre-line at an angle, the elbow connects with and deflects the opponent's arm away from your centre, while your forearm, hand and fingers line up straight out and at the opponent's face. If they continue the forward movement with their shoulder, you can simply slide your forearm up their arm and strike them in the neck or head.

The focus is on the wrist, which is pressed down as the hand moves into the Wu Sao structure. If the opponent tenses their arm as the Jum Sao is applied, their force will be attacking upwards into thin air, so you are free to simply thrust your fist forwards. As with all the structures in the system, if the opponent resists them in the wrong direction, you are free to hit.

This action can also be used to control an aggressive action. For example, if you have your right arm extended with your hand on the opponent's chest as though keeping them at arms length, if they attempt to attack you with their left arm you can sink the Jum Sao over their arm, deflecting their attack.

Protecting Prayer Palm/Wu Sao

The rear guard hand is held a fist distance from the centre of your chest, again in the prayer palm position; it has a forwarding energy that helps prevent it from being trapped against your body. Anything attempting to press it at your chest will force it into the next best position or structure for defence or offences. If your hand or arm gets pinned to your body, you must create a space to get out of the situation, using leverage, turning and flowing into an alternative structure or by stepping away from your trapped arm. As a stand alone structure, it is the last line of defence before your torso is contacted by an incoming strike. The Wu Sao position principles can also be used with a clenched fist or other tool or can simply be thrust forward and used as an attack with the hand edge. Defensively, as with Man Sao, it is the entire forearm, from elbow to hand edge that can be used to defend against an incoming strike.

Hook Hand/Fook Sao

Catch and detain an opponents arm or leg, use it like you are swatting a fly. Used as a hook when bridging the opponent's wrist, it can be applied to the inside or outside of their arm, and used to drag their attacking line down, exposing their throat.

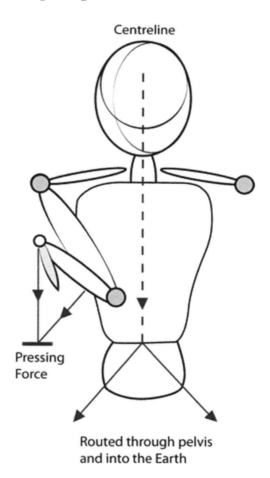

Centreline

Pressing
Force

Routed through pelvis
and into the Earth

This structure is thrown forward with the elbow moving through the inner triangle to centre, and the wrist thrown down the outer triangle to catch the incoming arm. With the elbow moving first, it should always beat the attackers punch to its position and once on centre it will deflect any force connecting with the elbow.

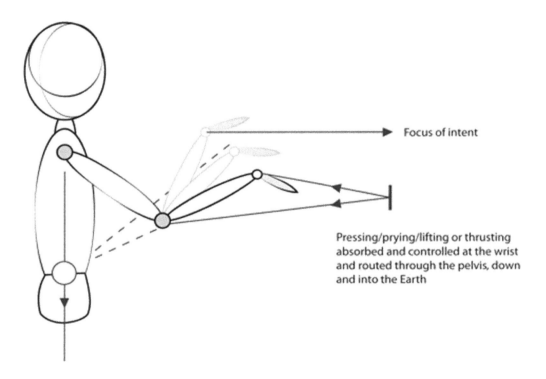

Focus of intent

Pressing/prying/lifting or thrusting absorbed and controlled at the wrist and routed through the pelvis, down and into the Earth

The forearm being relaxed moves forward with speed as the elbow thrusts it forward to catch the opponent's wrist. If the elbow in this shape connects first, you do not need the hand shape, so your hand is free to hit. If the wrist connects and the hook is applied, it detains their arm just long enough to lead them into another action to take their centre; i.e. Huen/Jum/Jut, etc.

Fook Sao covers the opponent's wrist or ankle. By placing your hand over the top of the opponent's wrist, your elbow, wrist and hand energy focuses forward to the opponent's solar plexus, if the opponent should thrust their hand forward and your hand fails to detect its movement, your elbow will deflect the majority if not all of the strikes force off away from your centre as it is held on centre. If they attempt to strike high, your wrist and forearm will deflect or dissolve their arms force by pressing slightly inward at their centre. If they attempt to come around your arm, your hand is again free to strike.

Slap Hand/Pak Sao

This action is used primarily as an angled slapping, palming or pressing action to deflect an incoming strike. Although it can be applied at any angle, when in the square facing/Doi Ying position, it is most effective when used as a slanting forward palm strike that crosses the centre-line on the way to the opponent's head.

If this action connects with the opponent's arm as they thrust at you, it will adhere to and parry their attack off to the inside gates/Noi Mun.

Depending on the amount of force used, the Pak Sao will either come to rest on the centre-line between you and the opponent or it will be forced back into the position you press to in the Sui Lum Tao form, with the elbow of the structure on centre. If the opponent's force is strong, their contact with your hand or arm in the Pak Sao structure will force your forearm to pivot at the elbow, which will deflect their incoming arm, all the way to your shoulder if necessary. If their intention is weak, you will deflect their arm effortlessly and can then continue forward to strike.

As an offensive action the Pak Sao can be thrust out with tremendous force. If the opponent is attacking from the side it can be thrust into them as a strike following the sideward path it follows in the Sui lum Tao form. Continuing its extension, it becomes the position learned in the Chum Kui form. This striking with more power as it is extended from the waist rotation.

Pak Sao should connect to the wrist when applied to the inside of the arm, and the elbow, when applied to the outside of the arm. This then prevents the opponent continuing forward with a flowing counter move. It is also used to control both the opponent's arms at once, with your hand controlling one of the opponent's arms, and your forearm and elbow controlling the other, as in the example images.

Palm Strikes/Jin/Wang/Dai Jeung

These palm striking actions attack the opponent's groin, side, elbows, knees, neck, head and face. Jeung refers to palm striking actions in general. In the first instance, the palm is held with the fingers pointing to the sky, the palm heel driven forwards. Variations on this are striking with the palm edge, driven forwards by the elbow which simultaneously cuts onto the centre-line, deflecting anything that may exist along that line that may have been thrown at you by the opponent.

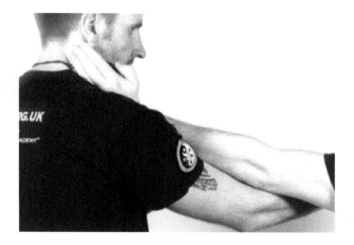

In reverse, it can be used to draw grabbing or clutching hands back and past the outside line of the body, reducing their effective ability to be used as a counter. The palms must be used correctly in relation to targets, the half circle teaches the correct application. Palm high, fingers point up, palm to midsection, fingers point to the side, palm low, fingers point down. This rule ensures minimum risk of injury to the hand and arm.

Repelling Hands/Gum/ Soh Sao

This action is used primarily to press or pin an opponent's structures or to create a space between you and the opponent as they try to control your arms for joint manipulation or grappling. Through extended resistance you can generate powerful striking actions that flow from Gum Sao. The Gum Sao are practiced in form in a sequence that trains the pressing force from the four directions, left, right, back and front. This allows the practitioner to press down on an opponent that may attack from a low position. Pressing down onto the top or side of their head keeps them at a safe range and makes it impossible for them to grab at your body, as does pressing forward and down onto their shoulders, sinking them into the floor. It can also apply to trapping actions in Kum Na where Pressing Energy/Bik Ging is required.

If you lock your arms out as you apply this, once their forward pressure is connected through to your stance and you have absorbed it, simply rotating your torso will cause them to move off in a direction away from you or drop them onto the floor. Alternatively, it will force them to move your entire bodyweight, which will cause fatigue in them. When applying Gum Sao, your bodyweight can be sunk down further and through the opponent's body.

We react to trapping and joint manipulation by understanding the positions we can be locked into. Then as we get a feel for the technique we can use the concept in this movement to move out of the attempted technique and recover facing, bringing our fists back into the fight.

Trapping is an element of Wing Chun that is important to understand. We do not try to trap or think about applying a trapping action, but when an opponent leaves their arms crossed, using the concept Lien Sui Dai Da, you will trap their arms without looking for it, they cannot continue their intended attack and you can finish the fight.

Although the basic aim of Wing Chun is to strike whenever possible, it is important to train trapping skills, then are aware when these actions are being applied to you. Some exponents can perform these skills very subtly, you should strive to understand the basic applications of leverage and joint manipulation at the very least.

One big reason trapping skill should be researched is that it is not always appropriate to use striking against someone out of control, your job may require you to have skill in control and restraint. As your skill in Wing Chun improves, it should be less likely that you will ever have to use it ruthlessly. Trapping in this respect being the more moral approach to self defence.

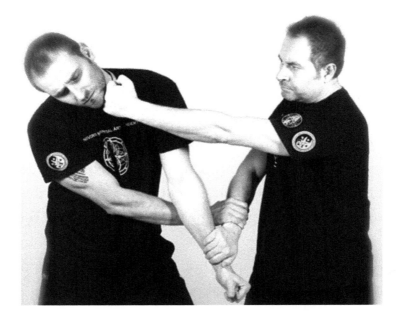

In the next image, the opponent grabs our Man Sao and attempts to strike the body, we rotate the waist sharply and use the strength of the opponents grip on our wrist to pull them forwards and into a powerful Low Palm/Dai Jeung.

Bar Arm//Lan Sao

This action deals with any pressing force by first absorbing it, then redirecting it. It can be used as a strong barrier between you and your opponent or to create space when pressed.

Lan Sao is followed by the Jam Sao in the form sequence, which sinks the elbow and diverts any pressing force away from your centre. If the action is pressed from the side, you angle the elbow being pressed downward which will redirect the pressing force through your stance and allow your Fak Sao to strike, the release of this resistance will lend a whipping force to the action.

If pressed from the front, dropping into Jam Sao will divert the prying force out at an angle to the left or right side of the stance, allowing you to take centre. This shape can also be used as a choke or throw.

In the image, it is applied to cover and sink an opponent's arms when they attach to your chest. Sinking their arms exposes their neck.

Chopping Arm/Fak Sao

The Fak Sao is thrown forward with energy starting at the elbow. The elbow moves forward and upward as the hand is thrust forwards, towards the target. If your elbow is pressed towards your face by the opponent, you can rotate the elbow down; this will draw the opponent into the Fak Sao structure as you throw it out. As this happens, the opponent's force is being redirected through your stance and into the floor. The Fak Sao is useful for covering a large target area, 90° from an outstretched arm or 180° if starting the action with your hand close to your chest.

This hand shape can be thrust directly at the opponent in front. It can also be thrown out in an arch, either to strike the opponent or to deflect an incoming attack.

The Fak Sao action is particularly useful against circular strikes as it can punish the arms of the attacker. It can also be used to find and connect to an opponent that may have side stepped you or been attacking from the side.

It is a very powerful strike in real application. In a ground fighting position, this action trains the hinging strike at the elbow, which can be combined with a Fung Nan Choi or Gurn Choi strike to the opponent's head, neck and body.

In the example the opponent has attacked from our side. The elbow of the Fak Sao connects to the opponents arm, and with power from the waist rotation, discussed later, we lever their arm off our centre with powerful waist rotation and hack the neck with the hand edge.

Slicing Arm/Jam Sao

In this action, the elbow moves through the inner triangle, the wrist slices down the outer triangle. As it intercepts the opponents arm it redirects their attacking force down towards your elbow, as it does you detach and strike. Your elbow should be punched along the inner triangle line, that way, even if the opponent is close to landing their strike, you will intercept it at the wrist, their strikes weakest point, this applies to many of the actions learned.

Jerking Arm/Jut Sao

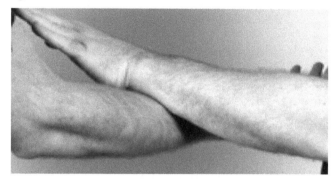

This action is used with the wrist held at an angle higher than the elbow to draw or dissolve an attacking force across the body or into the stance. It can be used to draw the opponent's fist low and across centre, or used to deflect their entire arm off centre. As the elbow is drawn back at an angle and into the centre, the wrist moves across the centre, connecting with the attacker's incoming arm and then jerking it down and across the body, the fingers of the Jut Sao hand continually pointing at the opponent's throat. If the opponent over commits with their forward movement or balance, they will fall into the counter move which can simply be a thrusting finger or hand strike. This structure can also be applied with a forward force, or to the back or side of an opponent's neck, chopping back at an angle with devastating effect.

If the opponent should grab you, strike them. If they are attempting to grab you, use the Jut Sao action to divert their grabbing arm, before it makes contact. This will lead them effortlessly into the Bui Sao counter move, while they are still thinking about the grab.

Best used when your arm is already extended, as in the example with Jum Sao, if you are attempting to keep someone at arms length, and they then make a move at you, you can use this structure to great effect. It can also be used to strike an opponent if you have them in a rear neck lock or choke, striking them with the wrist and palm heel. The feeling when applying Jut Sao is chopping.

Thrusting Arm/Bui Sao

The arm is thrust forward to intercept and deflect anything that has either taken the centre line, or is thrown through an arc. As a hook punch is thrown with force, the Bui Sao must be projected to its full extent and held firm with long energy while the power driven at it is dissolved.

If using the Finger Thrust/Bui Jee, the fingers should be held firmly together to give them structural support. Awareness of the power comes from the palm heel, which then presses energy into the hand and up into the fingers as the hand is thrust forward. As it hits, the energy passes out and into the opponent. It can be used as a method of snaking around the opponent's structures.

High Bridging Arm/Ding Sao

This action can be used to defend quickly if you attempt to strike high, and notice the attacker has a knife which they thrust in low at you. You can quickly whip your hand down in the straight or semicircular action and deflect or pin it. Vice versa if you go for a low attack or counter as the opponent changes direction and attacks high, you can quickly throw your wrist up. The wrist strike can also be used if you have injured your hand or fingers, swinging it at the centre just like the Fak Sao.

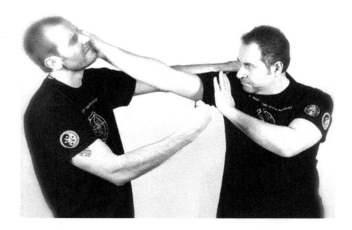

Cultivating Hand/Gwat Sao

Executed through an arc, down and sideward, covering the lower gates, this action can also be used to chop at the limbs of the opponent as they attack. A kick or punch to your stomach, or the side of the head of an opponent coming in low to grapple you, can all be smashed with this action. Against other skilled opponents, the sideward action can slingshot their low strike up and back around at your head, here we combine the Gahn and Jam Sao action to counter.

From a bridged position over the opponents arm we start this action by drawing the elbow back toward the hip through a small arc, while the wrist and hand cover the lower left or right gates. As your bodyweight is already sunk over your elbow, if the opponent is using force from their shoulders to push their strike home, you can drag them out of position and take their balance.

Wing Arm/Bong Sao

Fig 1.1 Shows the initial bridging position between the opponents attacking limb and the Bong Sao structure. If no pressure is applied the structure can remain in the ready position.

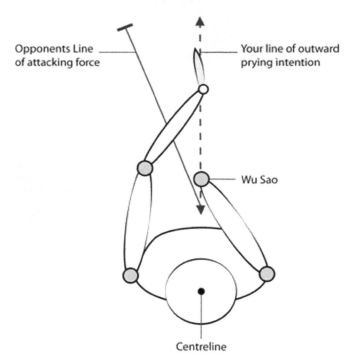

Birdseye view of Bong Sao

The basic idea of this position is to deflect incoming striking force to the side, with a recoiling force being used effectively to strike back at the opponent from the same position. This is achieved when the hand and forearm of the Bong Sao action strikes up from underneath, rising up at an angle to the chin or neck area of the opponent. If nothing gets in its way the side of the hand or forearm strikes the opponent/Fak Sao. If the Bong Sao is bridged, and if the bridging force is greater than the force of the Bong Sao going out, it will force your elbow across your body at an angle to the users centre, which then makes it a diverting movement. As soon as the elbow of the Bong Sao has moved towards the users centre, the structure is no longer required, you have their centre.

Fig 1.2 Shows the Bong Sao forced across the chest by the opponents attack and the deflection of the opponents attacking limb to the outside line. The Wu Sao now ready to attack down the centreline, freeing the Bong Sao position.

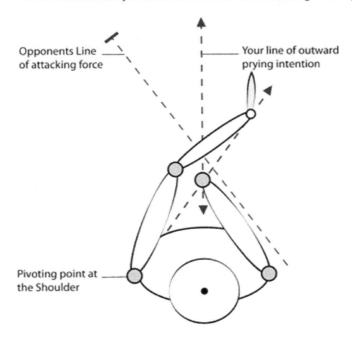

Opponents Line of attacking force

Your line of outward prying intention

Pivoting point at the Shoulder

Birdseye view of Bong Sao

When bridged you should focus on striking with the hand of the Bong Sao structure, this creates the feeling of spring force, the arm is thought of as a length of bamboo, which when bent, flexes energy as it tries to recover its original shape. If the opponent disconnects from your Bong Sao, your forward energy will project your arm forwards and they will be hit. If they press their wrist or elbow onto your Bong Sao you can comfortably receive and absorb that force while allowing the Bong Sao structure to rotate off centre at your shoulder, deflecting the incoming energy safely to the side of your body without shape collapsing.

This is one of the most misunderstood actions in Wing Chun with many accounts of people injuring their shoulders when trying to apply this action, due to a lifting the elbow and not driving it. If you lift the elbow of this structure with your shoulder, into an incoming downward movement, the downward force will win and tear your shoulder muscles. If force is applied to your arm in this direction, collapse to Tan Sao.

Using Bong Sao correctly, you must have focused intent on striking with the hand and forearm and let the opponents energy lead the Bong Sao movement every time, unless you are drawing or stepping in behind the Bong Sao, pressing the opponents torso in order to use Yi Bong.

If you use an upward chopping action from the elbow, with forward force from the elbow, anything you meet will be either lifted out of your way, or will force the correct deflection through the Bong Sao structure at the shoulder. If the opponent's pressing force is stronger, it will force your Bong, at the shoulder, to divert their energy off to the side, at which point you can regain centre by bridging with your other arm while simultaneously dropping the Bong Sao structure into a ready position.

Practice throwing the Bong Sao with a relaxed wrist, the hand will rotate downward as you extend the arm and the structure in contact will feel relaxed.

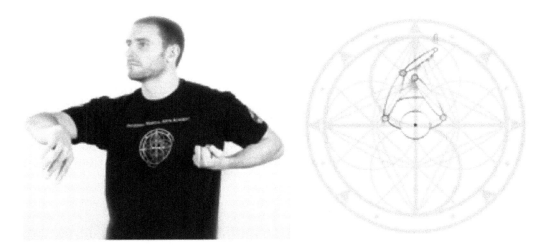

When you understand this position you will flow effortlessly from Tan Sao to Bong Sao and back to Tan Sao when the opponent applies the corresponding energy.

Uplifting Arm/Tok Sao

Uplifting refers to the direction of energy. This action is performed by thrusting the palm heels forwards and upwards at an angle to the opponent's face, the palm heels are supported by the elbows which are supported by the pelvis and stance. Energy from the stance is thrust upwards while the elbows are tucked in close to the body, this energy continues through the hands which travel forwards and up from under the opponent's arms.

To generate more force you can also pivot the forearms back through towards your chest while keeping your elbows static, this creates an arcing force that throws the opponent's hands up and away and can cause their arms serious damage. If someone attempts to push or grab you, this action is very effective in countering.

Changing Hands/Tut Sao/Chan Sao

This action teaches force generation, the principle of separating the elbows or changing the forward position and rear hand positions, creating an instinctive response to an attempted trapping of your arms. These actions can be applied at any angle in relation to the opponent and also teach the positions for basic joint locks.

When performing these actions, we are reminded that the elbows should constantly be working with opposing force. As one elbow travels forward, for the most part, the other is travelling backwards. This concept will reinforce the idea of the elbows never moving in one direction together, which prevents your wrists from easily being crossed or pinned. With one elbow held back, there is always a hand to strike with and we avoid basic trapping.

Linked Rapid Punches/Lin Wan Kuen

With the basic straight punch understood, we begin cyclic defensive and attacking punches. The defensive structure of the withdrawn punch is angled, the fist turned up to increase the deflective width of the wrist, the elbow held downward and outward near the hip creating an angled deflecting forearm. The withdrawn fist is held near the elbow of the extended arm. This provides a barrier against any strikes that may attempt to strike from underneath your extended arm. If this happens, on feeling contact with the opponents striking wrist, you should immediately drive your elbow forwards and thrust your fist into your opponents centre.

If your opponent punches over the extended arm, the withdrawn punch moves through the centre, over your extended arm position and thrust forward at the opponent's centre, which simultaneously deflects the opposing incoming strike away from your centre, "The attacking hand is also the defending hand".

Chain punching is a highly effective and basic method of defence through attack that will be difficult to deal with when executed quickly.

Train until you can perform fifty punches in around five to six-seconds for speed training. Then train to throw twenty powerful punches in around the same amount of time. Speed without power is useless. When you hit, keep hitting the target until it moves out of range, keep the arms extended to guard against any flailing energy that may still be thrown at you and move forward and back into striking range to hit again.

Once you have understood chain punching, always lead with this when no bridge exists between you and your training partner, you will then force each other to deal with the most efficient methods of striking, learning to competently and confidently move forward, bridge, sink and deflect strikes from your centre.

Although a single straight thrust punching is not as powerful as a western boxing straight cross, it makes up for this shortfall in power by the number of punches that can be thrown in the same period of time. The first punch stops the opponent in their tracks, the second drives the full impact force through the head, and the third knocks them out. Train to hit the same point over and over again.

Keep the body relaxed yet strong, and use dynamic tension at the end of each movement. Drive aggressive intent home with the correct attributes in place. Pull the withdrawing elbow back and down with power, anything under it will be dragged from centre.

Expanding concepts in Chum Kui

When we come to Chum Kui, we have already learned and established the principles and concepts of the Sui Lum Tao form. Our arms structures are well set, correctly positioned through the stance to absorb force. We can deal with and deflect huge thrusting and pressing forces applied at our centre. Here, we focus on staying on the outside of the opponent's arms to give us maximum control over their centre of balance and their reserve striking arm. If an opponent keeps their first strike extended and attempts to then strike with their other hand, we tie them up, crossing the arms.

The focus of your intent or mind is always at the opponents centre. If they keep pressing forward you deflect or uproot them. Combinations of striking and deflecting applications are also practiced. Again, with the focus on staying more to the outer three gates side of the opponent. Hand structures like Tan Da are extended forward at the opponent's incoming arm. In Chum Kui, due to the ability to use torso rotation, these actions become stronger and more subtle.

Exercises at this stage can develop further with the introduction of footwork. Dan Chi Sao with turning, improving the effectiveness of your structures and testing them to their limits. In drills, we strive to constantly improve our feeling and technical ability and use of the system.

Understanding this form bring the movements already learned in Sui Lum Tao to life. With the introduction of torso rotation, footwork and kicking, the form teaches us how to stay on an opponents centre or turn to face them while remaining relaxed, balanced and coiled, effectively

Chum Kui turns you into a human gun turret. This method is highly efficient as it does not require you to use over complicated footwork to follow an opponent circling you. You learn to turn through 180 degrees with speed, able to whip the body from right to left in a split second. We learn how to hit with the whipping action of the waist, throwing power through the elbows and extend the energy into punches, palms and chopping actions. We also develop the understanding of fighting ranges and how to break them down and reconstruct them efficiently.

Rotation through the basic stance allows you to efficiently track an opponent that moves around you. Just standing and rotating the torso conserves energy, keeps you balanced and calm and does not draw you into the opponents fight plan.

The form teaches us how to step while generating force in any direction, rotate to track an opponent and turn with torquing power while remaining balanced and grounded, as well as introducing kicking and using the legs in rotation to deflect kicks. Torso rotation develops power used to move or throw an opponent that is very close to us. We train footwork for dynamic movement through kicking, angled stepping, facing and shuffling.

When the time to move comes, because you are forced back or need to move forward to continue the fight, this forms teachings are utilised. From the stance, if we are pressed back by the opponent, we drop back into a fighting stance, one leg forward, one leg back. From here, any further pressure from the opponent is rooted into the rear supporting leg, at which point we have recovered our balance and are ready to continue the fight from a stronger stance.

From the forward or lead position, if our opponent continues to press us we can root that force through our rear leg, and kick with the lead, while using the opponent's resistance to remain balanced and upright. This method is very effective if both your hands are bridged with the opponents, as you can use your foot or leg to attack their groin, feet, knees and shins, forcing them to divert their attention to their lower body, at which point, your hands will find their targets.

Footwork should be understood as where the opponent has moved you to. If you can stand your ground, do so. If they come charging in, sidestep. If they shove you, rotate and deflect or drop back into the next strongest position and stance. Footwork moves through five basic directions. Back left, back right, forward left, forward right and forward centre. Try to avoid moving straight because if the opponent follows you, they build mass in their bodyweight that could knock you off balance.

The stepping actions are performed by lifting one leg of the rooted stance off of the floor, at which point the supporting leg springs you forward or backwards depending on which leg is lifted. Each time you step and arrive at the next point, simply turning your foot inwards takes you back into the basic stance.

Which direction you want to move in, is determined by the distribution of weight over the supporting leg. If you want to spring forward, you move bodyweight over the ball of the supporting foot, then as you lift the advancing leg the supporting leg will propel you in that direction, this is fairly simple to understand but takes a lot of training to apply instinctively.

To do this correctly, the body structure power is held in the lower abdomen, and connected to the elbows and knees. Used correctly, it will propel the correct leg forward or backward in relation to where you are being pulled or pushed. If pulled excessively hard, you can take the opponent's balance by crashing into them, either with your head, body, arm or leg.

Holding energy through the body in this way ensures footwork becomes powered by external resistance, 'the enemy leads you to a better position'. If you are pulled or pushed, your torso will not bend forwards, instead, your waist is shifted and the corresponding leg is lead into a balanced and forward fighting position.

Your body weight gives you the proper resistance to the ground and therefore good connection to the ground, it is this resistance that you use to move yourself dynamically. Basic stance training will make your legs strong and when you keep the knees sprung, you will move with power. Once understood, this ability allows you to put your whole bodyweight behind the actions of your arms and hands, lending more force to everything you do.

The stance when turning is utilised one leg at a time. If we are pressed from the front, the rear leg absorbs the force. If we are pressed from the back, the force is absorbed in the front leg, if we are pulled forward by our lead arm, we can ground this force through the front leg, build up resistance and then spring out at the opponents centre, borrowing the opponents pulling force, doubling our strikes penetrating power.

When turning, striking force is generated by rotating the torso and thrusting the striking tool into the target, the feel for striking power coming from the wall bag. This is the same for the kicking actions. When we are kicked by the opponent, we can deal with it by either thrusting our leg out to kick their leg, or lifting our knee at their centre, allowing their kick to strike the sole of our foot.

At the Chum Kui level we can bridge to the opponent by striking out with the arms and the leg at the same time. This makes your attack difficult to counter, if the punch is stopped, the kick will get through and vice versa.

The circular energy developed at this stage also teaches us how to generate hooking strikes and powerful uppercuts, recover facing and apply greater leverage for limb destruction. These applications can be utilised when this form has been understood and so the practitioner is not limited in their striking application, which gives us more tactical options.

The ability to absorb force while rotating and throwing it back at the opponent is known as the slingshot effect and generates a lot of striking power. To effect this kind of power, your strike must be moving through a relaxed and flowing line of force that is thrown from the waist.

With the body weight held in your elbow, all your body goes into applying leverage at the elbow joint, which is then difficult to lift when countering. Understanding this will improve your joint locking techniques.

Pressing power/Bik Ging is developed and becomes another natural extension of your body movement. If the opponent does not have a strong stance, you can simply step into them and take their balance.

With your moving stance power and body structure behind the push or strike, everything arrives at once and the opponent is moved effortlessly away.

When an opponent moves into attack, we learn to absorb just the right amount of force to get the opponent to stick to us in order to effectively put the opponent in the wrong position. To achieve this we make the opponent resist us is one of the eight direction, this sends their arm away from your centre when you disconnect to attack them. This is why flowing is so important. If you stop and stay in any position too long, your opponent can get a feel for where your intention is, and can therefore turn the advantage to their favour.

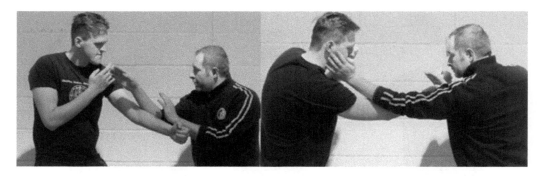

When you have a line on the opponent, you thrust your hands forwards. If they have a structure in front of that line, you will connect to their arms. When connected, you can still press your intention home. This will increase the pressure between your arms. Pressing from the ground, you build up power at the point of contact. At this point, if they disconnect, your hand will shoot forwards and hit them. If there force becomes to strong and your structure begins to fail, you can rotate your torso structure, which will draw the opponents' force around you.

There are many methods of redirecting and dissolving force pressed at you. One is to hold off the structure with your own, then briefly collapse back. This will cause the opponent to disconnect briefly and then chase your arm. At the point where they catch up with your arm again, you begin to rotate its position to cause the desired deflection. Another is as already stated, to rotate the torso, elbow and arm position. You can combine the two methods seamlessly, as the opponent is diverted, if they are pressing heavily on you, as they fall forwards, you can thrust your arm up at centre again and they will simply crash into your strike as it goes out, doubling its power.

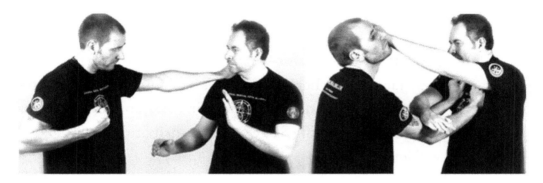

All the structures in the system can have weight and power allied to them. Either your bodyweight and pressing power can be put behind the movements, or sunk on top of them to put your bodyweight onto the opponents arms, causing them collapse or lift to resist you, which wears them down.

Ding Sao

Thrusting this action forward and upward as in the first form, we aim to strike out with the palm heels while driving our thumbs and fingers down at an angle. Imagining that you are thrusting your thumbs into the eyes of the opponent to give the hands the correct distance from each other. The fingers can also be thought of as striking down into the opponent's neck.

There are two actions taking place when doing this in form. The initial action is Seung Jam Sao, where the elbows cut into centre over the opponents arm, then we thrust the Ding Sao. In application, if an opponent grabs you, thrust Ding Sao out under their arm and straight to target, they will let go.

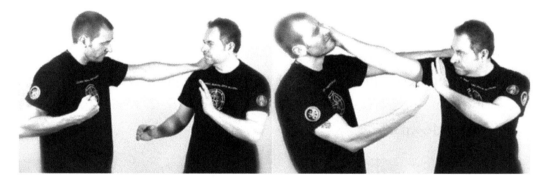

The palm heels can also strike the opponents face and head. If both hands are used at once it can be used to grab and control the opponents head, pressing it back, pulling it forwards or moving it to the sides, the hands can also grab the opponents ears and be used to control the head that way. If an opponent has grabbed you from the front, this is a good structure to use to break their grip and pull them into a throw or strike.

Hacking Elbow/Pai Jarn

The energy originates at the waist and is projected through the opponent from the feet, the elbow is hacked into the target. When practicing in form, as we move into this action, the right hand swings the elbow round to rest over the top of the left hand. Palms facing the floor. As you turn, focus power at the back of the left elbow as though striking with it, then as you come to arrive into the turned stance, focus striking power at the front of the right elbow. As you begin to turn with these actions, it is also important to angle your elbows down slightly, this takes care of any attempts to lift or press the structures in order to uproot your position, as well as drive power of the elbow strikes down into the opponent, by lending your torso body weight to the turn.

When turning, another key issue is to remain balanced and upright with pressing power from your stance held equally between the legs. If your back is pressed on centre, this turning action can deal with the pressing force very effectively, while bringing the opponent into striking range.

Trapping Arms/Jip Sao

Drawing the right hand over and the left hand pressing up. This action which combines the Tok Sao and Jut Sao movements with Bik Ging, teaching a method for trapping, rotating and catching.

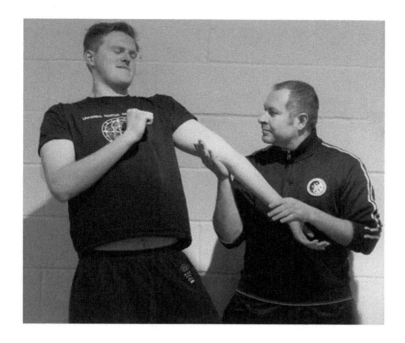

It can be applied to a foot, Knee, leg, arm and also to the head. Controlling the opponents head to disorientate or break the neck. After performing this action we move into the palm striking actions then draw the elbow back as we rotate our torso and end in the Lan Sao position.

When practicing, learn to press the downward palm onto the uplifting elbow, this resistance builds the upper body further and becomes another exercise in power development. This idea can be found in many areas of form practice.

Thrusting Palms/Jic Jeung

The palms are thrown from the waist rotation and line up with the opposite shoulders. Teaching the concept of striking past centre to the position a side stepping attacker is moving to. This is known as Striking the Shadow/Da Yeung. Another important aspect of this angled palm is for application on an opponent that is in elbow range.

Applying the palm to the side of the opponents head will give you a better opportunity of breaking their balance, as you are not pressing directly through their stance, but are instead pressing through the cervical joints in the neck. The neck comfortably collapses backwards but when done at speed can cause whiplash. From the side the neck is vulnerable and can be broken easily if sudden pressure is applied.

Bar Arm/Lan Sao

In this position, the forearm is held horizontally with the elbow angled down slightly. This structure can be used to press the opponent back, force them away if they are attempting to control your elbow from the side or rammed into the head of an opponent coming in low at you. Structurally it is very strong if pressed at the right point. Primarily in the form, it can be used to test your grounding and the ability to shift weight onto the rear leg, freeing up the front leg for kicking. It can also be used as a way of keeping an opponents pressing force at the periphery of your spherical defence. The hand position in Lan Sao can be any structure that can strike, e.g., fist or palm. If done while receiving and sinking the opponents energy, you can lead then straight onto the striking tool on the end of the Lan Sao structure.

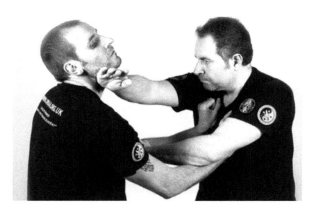

Yielding Wing/Yi Bong Sao

This action can be used to rotate any pressing force away from your centre, either by moving the Lan Sao to Bong Sao or vice versa. When rotating back to Lan Sao, the Wu Sao is drawn back through the rear elbow strike to create space around you and is an excellent way to escape from someone attempting to restrain you, this expands on the idea of the opposing elbows in the first form.

In practice you can play with variants of deflection through the Bong Sao, by throwing it forward on a straight line, curving it out and back, allowing it to fold inwards or striking with it.

Ascending Heel Kick/Dang Gurk

Section two in the form teaches us the first kicking action. It is thrust upwards, driving the heel forward.

As the kick descends it draws the bodyweight forward adding weight to the action of scraping the opponents shin and stamping onto the instep. As the kicking foot is placed on the ground the Pau Bong and Wu Sao are thrown out. Used as a method to regain the bridge safely, either moving at or away from the opponent.

Hook Punch/Cho Kuen

As well as showing you how to strike from the Bong Sao structure, you are also cutting across centre with the elbow and developing driving and striking force into the uppercut and circular principles of movement.

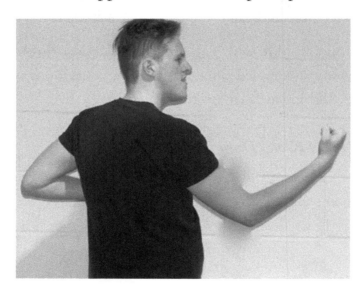

This action can therefore deflect and strike in one motion, like the thrusting punch. It can also flow into the lifting elbow if the fist misses the target.

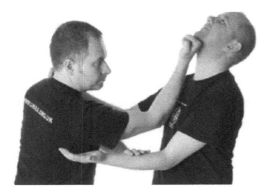

The Cho Kuen can be used from any angle and when done in form, should be combined with torso rotation for added force generation.

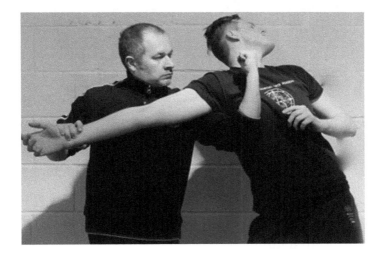

When testing the Cho kuen action, be sure to train the ability to press resisting force down and then up smoothly from the back foot through the elbow and wrist.

Once the structural power is understood, learn to throw curved striking actions smoothly from any position. These strikes can be hard to detect and therefore find the target more frequently, and hit with a lot of force.

Recover Facing/Yi Ying Sao

From the Cho Kuen action, we rotate the torso square on while simultaneously applying the Jum Sao, ending in the Wu Sao structure. This elbow rotation redirects any pressure up and round to the floor, and is applied from many positions. Known and Yi Ying Sao, it helps us to face the opponent if the attack or restraint comes from our side.

We simply rotate using the Yui Ma, while keeping our arms back in the withdrawn elbow position. Here you can think of it as just deflecting someone that is pressing on your torso. After we turn, we can punch them or kick out thrusting the heel forward. When kicking, train to line the heel of your kicking foot up with the knee of your supporting leg, that way, anyone attacking your supporting leg will be kicked or deflected by your attacking leg.

The concept of Yi Ying Sao is constantly occurring in Chi Sao as one aim of the exercise is restricting your partner's position and ability to stay facing your six gates by leading them into crossed arm positions.

Low Wing Arm/Dai Bong Sao

With this Bong Sao action, still think of chopping outwards and upwards. Anything moving in low at you in application will be deflected by this action. Low Bong can be used to deflect or strike something very close to your lower torso.

After the Dai Bong are performed, we bring the hands back up, rotating them through Tan Sao. At their simplest, these actions can be used to charge into someone attempting to restrain you by the arms. Used together, the actions of Tan and Dai Bong Sao create Kwun Sao.

The Dai Bong Sao is usually pulled into position by the opponent dragging your wrist downward. To avoid damage to the shoulder, you allow the arm to move in the direction of the pulling force, while your rear hand counters the strike.

Double Jerking Arms/Double Palms/Seung Jut Sao/Seung Jic Jeung

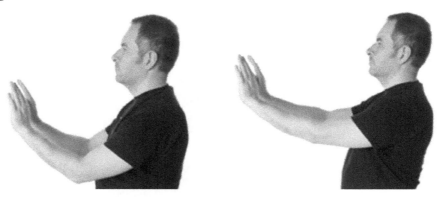

Here you can imagine an opponent controlling you by grabbing your chest. Simply placing your arms over theirs and sinking them through Jut Sao, you draw their torso forward, at which point you place your palms on their chest, let their bodyweight travel through your stance and then as they ground you, you propel them away powerfully. A characteristic of this action is to rise up by extending your legs as you push forward. This combines the extension of your arms and legs together creating a more powerful pushing or striking force which you learn to apply while keeping the body balanced and upright.

Additional Concepts in Bui Jee Form

8 Directional Elbows

Gwai Jarn/Diagonal Elbow

Kup Jarn/Pressing Elbow

Pie Jarn/Hacking Elbow

Tok Jarn/Uplifting Elbow

Train to strike with the elbows from left to right, up and down, diagonal high and diagonal low. Elbows are a powerful offensive and defensive tool. In defence, lead with an elbow held in front of your face, below the eye line, covering your nose. Moving forward, if the opponent jabs it, they injure their hand, if they strike around it, you can whip your wrist out from where the elbow is held and chop at them with your hand. It is a very effective tactic. When held up in front of your face, the shoulder and forearm protect both sides of the neck and can force an opponent to try and control it, at which point you could attack them.

Elbow tactics feature heavily in this third form, as well as movement for throwing, locking, sweeping. The main benefit of practicing this form is the amazing stretching it adds to your practice, the increased flexibility later adds to the power you can deliver through your movements and at the target.

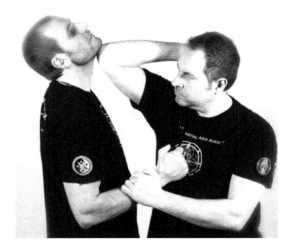

The power should be focused through rapid body movement and the energy extended to the very tip of the fingers, make every action has this feeling and you will gain even more from its practice.

Due to the importance of the elbow and its use throughout the forms, one aspect that this form deals with is the potential control by the opponent of our elbow. If it is pressed across our body we recover Doi Ying by using the Bui Sao action.

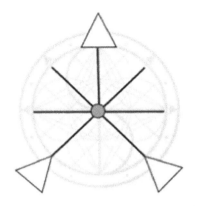

Grey Circle = Body Centre. Footwork.

*Forward from Centre.
*Centre from Forward.
Forward Right/Left from Centre.
Right/Left from Center.
*Back/Right from Centre.
*Back/Left from Centre.
*Centre/Back Left/Right from Forward.

 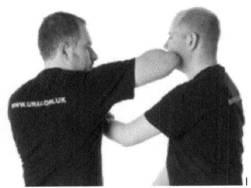

Saam Bai Fut/Three Bows to Buddha

The bowing actions teach us to cover the head with the elbows if pulled down or to recover to a standing position. We also develop flexibility that can be used to take the balance of an opponent attempting a rear choke, we can apply leg takedowns and sweeping. From an action that would appear simple, many tactical concepts can arise. This is the beauty of the system, once all the sum of its parts are understood, it becomes limitless in its application.

When looking at the Bui Jee form, we can see that emphasis is on extending the energy from the floor through the body at maximum acceleration. To do this, the body must become even more flexible.

'Wooden Man Post', 'Muk Yong Jong'

The form teaches you angling footwork, while driving power from the legs, through the arms and into the dummy core using all principles learned in the previous forms. When practicing, try and keep your eyes on the dummies centre at all times. Don't clash against its arms, instead, learn to connect and stick to the dummy arms and legs while focusing power through the dummies centre or shoulder lines.

Directional footwork is covered in depth when training the Jong. The diagram depicts the following steps that shift you from your starting position, in seven directions, just follow the arrow heads on the diagram below. Imagine yourself stood on the centre point of the diagram, the arrow heads then show you the direction of your step. The direction of the arrow head also shows you where your energy is focused. You exist in the centre of the diagram, and your opponent moves around the perimeter.

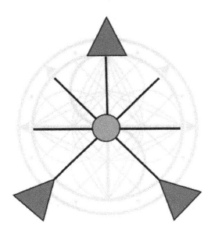

From a square on stance, first learn how to move forward on a straight line path. As mentioned earlier, if you imagine a triangle being drawn, your first step will be to the tip of that triangle. Moving either the right or left foot onto the tip of the triangle puts you into a forward fighting stance.

To make the movement more dynamic, perform the same action, only now, thrust yourself forward from the back foot as you just after your lead leg begins to move forward, this will shift your centre forwards further into the opponents centre.

Advancing forward footwork can be done in several ways. Moving down the centreline path being the most basic. Once understood, begin to practice moving diagonally. When moving across the opponents centre, aim to be on the outside of their attacking arm, this is known as moving to the '3 gate' position of the opponent. Effectively, the position the opponent find themselves in is limited, as only one side of their body is in the fight, while you can reach them with both of your arms and legs. Tactically, moving to the inside of the opponents attack gives them the ability to attack from the other side. If you move into the opponent this way, using diagonal footwork, aim to place your lead foot inside the position of their lead foot, making them unstable. This creates a problem for the opponents balance and prevents them from kicking or changing their angle to counter attack easily

The sequence below shows angling from centre to back left shift, back to centre then to back right shift.

Circular footwork/Sao Ma/Huen Ma involves stepping through half circles, this makes it difficult for the opponent to attack your legs as you move, and can be an effective way of catching and taking your opponents balance.

The double step is used when you have the opponent's balance, as they begin to buckle, simply make a second thrusting step and they will be projected away from you. Catching or hooking their ankle with your foot will flip them, stepping and staying on their foot before the action will drop them.

Kicking someone in the knees and shins or stamping on their feet when at punching range can be a highly successful tactic. The Shadowless kick/Mo Ying Gurk is impossible to see when fighting at close range or working from in a clinch, attacking the opponents lower legs with thrusting powerful digging kicks can destabilise the aggressor and take away their power when striking. When in striking range, sensing these kicks must be done through the sustained contact with the opponents arms.

Power is pressed, pushed, punched and kicked into the dummy with a flexible force that continuously flows from whichever position and arm structure you use to connect to it. Learn and drill the traditional form and then break it up, use your imagination and bring the dummy to life. All combinations of techniques can be applied with speed and power. The form keeps you working through the fundamental actions for applying Lin Sui Dai Da, evasive and pressing footwork, kicking and sweeping actions and efficient transitions from structure to structure. It also introduces new combinations of hand and leg applications as well as some new concepts.

Scooping Arm/Kao Sao

This is simply the Wing Arm/Bong Sao applied with the energy thrown through the forearm and out of the palm, in order to subtly redirect force off centre. It combines the movements of Huen Sao and Bong Sao energies.

Neck Detaining Arm/Kao Geng Sao

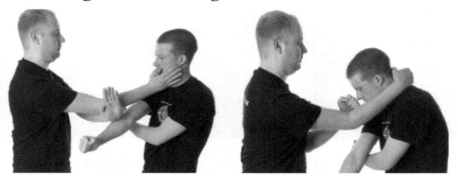

Pulling the neck occurs because our initial strike passes the head, either through the opponent shifting sideways or deflecting our arm. In application, the hand slaps and clamps onto the back of the head or neck as the elbow is snapped back violently, this action can cause severe damage to the neck, it is a good technique for dis-orientation and breaking the opponent's body structure.

Po Pai Jeung/Butterfly Palms

Used to recover balance when pulled by pressing at the opponents centre or to strike and push an opponent in any direction.

Baat Jam Dao/Eight Slashing Knives

A weapon adds range, and its own characteristics to your fighting capability. A bladed weapon gives you the ability to puncture or open up and opponent, causing blood loss and quick demise. You can remove limbs, crush skulls, break limbs and totally incapacitate an attacker.

There are actions within the form that throw centrifugal force, as a result of torso rotation, through the body, the faster you can move through each action, the lighter the knives become when thrown, yet heavier when they land. As you bring them under control, the resistance your muscles experience work the body hard. Practicing the knives can be an intensive workout in its own right. Heavier knives offer a greater workout.

Adding heavy weaponry to your training develops stance, waist & wrist power further, as well as the ability to apply "Killing Bridge". The way you use energy to kill with the knives, also translates into other weapons and applied to the forearms and hands when no weapon exists.

All the actions learned in the hand forms and dummy form can be found in the knife form and exercises. The more you practice with the knives in hand, the stronger your movements become.

Actions introduced and applied on the dummy such as Kwun Sao and Seung Gahn Jam Sao develop the waist power and body further when done with speed.

In terms of technical application, the first four-forms have taught you a number of varied applications, that can be combined together with speed, power and sensitivity to pressure. In the Baat Jam Dao form, power in the actions learned in the empty hand forms is developed further, as your body becomes stronger when controlling the weight of the blades in practice and throwing striking energy through them.

This is done by understanding the reaction to heavy flowing weight in technique, which forces a reaction that the techniques in the knife form continue to suppress and control. Without knowing these actions, you can still gain a great deal from just training the basic actions, which will strengthen your body and mind.

The knives therefore are thought of as a dynamic body building tool, but stay within the parameters of the system, being useful not just in power development, but also developing a serious mind. Knife fighting after all tends to have a serious outcome.

The actions of the form teach specific methods for dealing with long and short weapons. It also teaches us to move our body weight slightly further forward when moving, fast paced chasing and withdrawing footwork and precision in stabbing and slashing/punching and chopping.

They cut through the eight angles with speed and power. When we stab we punch and when we punch we stab, the movement and energy is the same, but the wrist is relaxed and the fist collapses when the blade stabs forward.

Luk Deem Boon Kwun/6½ Point Pole

This is a seriously underestimated training tool. Using the long pole teaches you the perfect timing for your striking energy, as well as being able to extend it further through the opponent. The Horse Stance/Sei Ping Ma is trained to add further flexibility and power into the legs using fa ging to propel us and our spearing. Moving the pole through an arc to snap down up or sideways requires full body power to do it with fast changes in direction. When learning the movements, if power is applied at the wrong moment, the pole will not move fluidly, and will always wobble at the tip. Each action should end with the pole held still and balanced, with focus on its point. Spend a minimum of five minutes without stopping working through the angles and understanding the application of all concepts learned, putting them into the pole when in practice.

Each action on the pole can hit the shadow, as the opponent moves, keep the pole on their centre, when they move in range, spear them.

Jin Kuen battle punches represent the final punch delivered in a fight, the one that is clear to hit and will finish the opponent. Practice from the horse stance and punch left then right while stepping. The Yui Ma and Jic Chung Choi energy are propelled and thrust from the step. Punch deep into the target, like thrusting the hand into wet sand, leave a deep and lasting impression. This then applies to all striking actions, when we find the maximum velocity for each action which is thrown like a whip.

Learning the sequences of all forms should be done thoroughly so you can derive all the benefits they give you, a healthy mind and healthy body.

"Knowing" forms

Knowing the sequence of the forms is not enough, this is the just the start. It is what is contained in the forms and the ability to apply the details that counts. Each action must be drilled many hundreds of times before it can be applied instinctively. There are no shortcuts to attaining skill, you must practice at every opportunity. To complete the first form is quite an achievement, you can remember the sequence, have an idea over the basic applications of each and every movement and are ready to move onto the next one.

When you practice form, you are engaged in a solo activity, designed to make an improvement to every facet of the fighting machine. It is your own personal exercise plan, so each time you practice, you should exert yourself. To my mind, the Wing Chun forms once understood are a complete workout, that you may only need to do once or twice a week for them to keep you fit and healthy. By the time you reach the stage in your practice where you know all the forms, you will know how to apply the first one to a high standard, fighting is a distant concept and a healthy mind and body are the reward. In summary then, the forms can be characterised as:

Sui Lum Tao

Developing the connected power in the legs and body through prolonged stance and posture training.

Learning to feel this connecting power between the joints while able to expand and contract it. Developing the concept of elbow energy or the "fixed elbow', connective power between the waist and elbow.

Forced mental focus on the power development in the knees and elbows through slow and strong flowing movement.

Basic stretching of the energy through the body that requires the correct feeling and mental intent.

Efficiency in striking/defensive strategy.

Learning to apply leverage.

Chum Kui

Developing the connected body power further by learning to channel energy through whipping force, thrown from waist rotation and footwork.

Developing the legs power further for kicking techniques, by driving the body sideways with power shifting and sitting on the back leg in practice you add more weight to the supporting leg and achieve a greater workout.

Bringing the Sui Lum Tao techniques to life through torso rotation, allowing you to drive power forward through striking actions while allowing you to stick to, control and yield to force that is pressed back at you. Learning to increase leverage for effective joint manipulation and throwing. Combined defence and attack 'Lin Sui Dai Da'.

This form will help you to adopt a more formal fighting posture and look, and disguise the power developed in the first form.

Bui Jee

Developing intent and the ability to direct energy with a firm and committed mind.

Extreme stretching. The power you have now practiced in the first two-forms will tighten the body, use the Bui Jee form to stretch it. Heightened feeling and awareness of the energy throughout the body, from toes to fingers, as you do every action with stretching in mind.

This form will increase your speed and the energy you deliver through your striking actions, develop greater accuracy in movement and a strong mental intent, as well as more fighting tactics and applications.

Muk Yong Jong Fut

Tests and develops the application of your bodies connected power through direct contact of techniques to an object with the ideal body structure. You can learn to test and apply all your striking force to its body while moving around and sticking to it with defensive positions.

This apparatus shows you where the weaknesses exist in your Wing Chun structure and allows you to correct them through feeling. None of your positions should collapse as you apply them to the Dummy, your body structure remains strong, and your energy focused and directed through its centre, it is an invaluable piece of training apparatus.

Baat Jam Dao.

Treat the knives as a body building tool. The additional weight but continued focus on combat orientated movement re-enforce the power you drive through your techniques when empty handed, as the form contains the actions from all form.

The Baat Jam Dao should be practiced with heavy knives and strong force in movement. It should feel like a workout training the back, waist, legs and arms. With the realistic applications in mind every cut should have the power to and decapitate.

Train with these in hand for 30 minutes each day. When you pick them up do not put them down for the entire time, just moving around with them in the beginning can be challenging. Once you have learned the forms and their applications, you can express the energy to apply the techniques from form, moving with speed and power and connecting the entire form together. A demanding and very satisfying workout.

You will quickly appreciate how useful a training tool these are if you use them right, and will notice huge increases in total body power and stamina.

Luk Deem Boon Kwun

Again, think of the pole form as a body building aid, one that tests your core strength and all attributes from the first five-forms. Each action executed with the long pole should be finely controlled, with the pole being still when held and smoothly, powerfully and efficiently moved in transition. The seven techniques develop internal power further. After working with the Long Pole, work speed and flexible power with the spear, it will feel light and portable, you will wield it with ease.

Your body structure is tested as the tip and weight of the long pole is always fighting your bodies alignment. You must keep the body straight and this takes work.

If you can go from the first form to last, in order and adding the correct idea to each, you have a serious workout regime, that will keep you fit and active your whole life.

Depending on what you want from your training, there are many levels of physical attrition that you can put yourself through to become the 'ultimate fighter'. Wing Chun offers methods that are more accessible to the majority of individuals that require highly advanced self defence/fighting skills and fitness training, without the rigours of cardiovascular, high intensity workouts that deviate from fighting theory.

The Wing Chun systems training also does not require the practitioner to spar or receive full blown repetitive strikes to the head and body. The focus is on valuing the commodity of the mind and protecting it from repeated traumatic striking force by dealing with an opponent, quickly, efficiently and with the minimum of physical effort, intelligent fighting.

There is a saying in Wing Chun, 'Glass head, bean curd body, iron bridges'. The head is your bodies control centre and therefore, extremely important. It should be thought of as very delicate, like glass, so you should not allow it to be hit. The mind and body are delicate; both are affected by the actions of others and so, should always be protected from negative physical and mental energy. This principle is the same for the body. You do not want to suffer internal injury, so contact to the body is also avoided as much as possible. In order to protect these valuable assets, you train your arms, hands, legs and feet to protect you like an iron shield.

On Multiple Opponents

If you are faced with more than one opponent, the first one that moves at you must be struck and put down quickly. If they don't go down, then you must hit them again. If you try to hold them or force them into a lock or throw, the situation will become hard to control, whoever you are and whatever you know. You won't have time to apply an arm bar lock when their companions are smashing chairs, bottles, ashtrays or fists into your face. Hold on to one for too long and the others may well take you down. By all means is you throw someone to the floor fine, but do not take them to the floor or you will be in trouble if they have company.

When dealing with multiple opponents you should attempt to herd them. Align yourself with the nearest aggressor and keep them as a barrier between you and the other opponents. Then knock them out in order of range.

Try to evaluate what there is around you, anything that can be used to even the odds should be acquired. A nearby wall or table can as already mentioned, be put to good use, either for slamming the opponent's head and body into, or throwing them over. Either way you buy yourself valuable time to get out of the situation alive and unharmed. If they bring the fight to you, and you absolutely cannot get out of there without a physical effort, then put your entire mind and body behind that effort.

In practice, train on pads, have a group of friends hold mitts and strike at them until you are exhausted. Train to hit hard and fast, with balanced accuracy, vocalise your aggression as you do so, as discussed earlier, get used to hearing your inner neanderthal. Fight as though the Baat Jam Dao are your arms, punch as though wielding the Long Pole. Striking somewhere on the body that is inherently weak will help you win the fight faster, a helpful approach when outnumbered.

A Fighting Stance

You may prefer to lead with your strongest and more natural side, your weaker side, or to stay square on. Whichever you prefer, you should train all methods of fighting stance and understand the strengths and weaknesses of each.

The benefit of training in the basic Square Facing/Doi Ying stance is that both sides of your body come together in their ability, so you feel comfortable leading with either hand, knowing that you have acquired the same ability on each side. Standing square on also offers no targets, which is important. An extended arm and hand, or knee, leg and foot can and will be attacked by someone that knows what they are doing. If you move from a square on stance straight into a flurry of punches, you never show your intention, which is much harder for an attacker to deal with. In self defence, raising your hands to a knife wielding attacker could cost you your fingers, open serious wounds to your wrists and vital areas, so don't offer them a target. If they are out of range, wait until they move in to strike you and go for it. Someone raising their fists at you shows you their intent, but also gives you a target. If their hand is the closest thing to you, strike it. Do it right and you can break the small bones in that hand, which is then no longer a threat.

Bridging Arms/Kui Sao

When we bridge arms with our training partner, we are connecting energies. We connect the arms and then feel the direction of our partner's incoming force, which is known as 'intention'. In the exercise of pushing hands, we look to bridge intention and continually keep it away from our centre of mass through deflection of the arms, moving them forward or backward, pressing up down and sideways, using torso rotation and shifting weight from one leg to the other. The idea is to keep the movement flowing, while simultaneously looking to keep our intention focused at our partner's centre of mass.

The feeling when controlling your partner's arms is equated to holding a ball. If your partner extends their arms forward while pressing your forearms, you will feel your arms being pushed back, you should train to give a small resistance to "stick" to their centre through their hands. Then train to resist more, to create a greater resistance in the partners hands, you can then learn to lead their energy off to the sides. Then move onto pressing, yielding and pressing again in fast succession. The exercise begins to resemble upright tag. When we have a partner pushing us, they provide the stimulus and energy we use to balance ourselves with.

Your training partners Slap/Pak Sao deflection should be structurally sound, so as to stop your thrusting or chopping arm from just crashing straight through and hitting into their neck. This should be trained well, if applied correctly, your training partner will feel immense force crashing into their slap deflection structure, as your whole body weight is behind your arm.

The moment your punch is stopped by the Pak Sao, you will feel the opportunity for your next position.

If the Pak Sao stops on your centre, change your punching arm to a Tan Sao and rotate your partners force off your centre, applying Tan Da. If the Pak Sao presses past the centre line, execute Lap Da. If the Pak Sao fails to stop your first punch, continue hitting centre.

Pull Hit/Lap Da

This exercise combines the concepts from the Bong/Wu/Lap/Fak /Tan/Pak Da, but primarily its focus is on the Lap Da/Bong Sao counter. Grabbing and pulling actions can be applied anywhere on the body and is highly effective when used on wrists, arms, the head and hair, the jaw and fingers. It can also be used to pull a weapon quickly from an adversary's hands.

In this cyclic drill, when your wrist is pulled, you use the momentum given by the training partners pull to throw your elbow forward and upwards to engage the incoming punch. Simply allowing your wrist to relax and rotate inward while driving your elbow at the opponents centre will create the correct angle for this action. If your elbow lines up with the opponents centre, you find the punching line, and strike through the elbow and then withdraw it, one hand back, one hand forward.

Always use this when your wrist is pulled in a horizontal direction away from your centre. If your wrist is pulled diagonal to the floor, you should not use this action as you will strain your shoulder, instead, use the Kwun Sao, if the opponent is just pulling you aggressively, you will be able to simply crash into the opponent with your body weight behind your shoulder, or change the Tan Sao position from Kwun into a strike.

The 'Bong Sao' is the first line of defence against the incoming punch when pulled. Once bridged and brought under control, the opponents punching arm, if presses back at your centre, becomes an obstacle to your counter strike, it needs removing.

To remove the obstacle and find the opponents centre, we challenge the punch by driving the wrist of our rear guard hand as though punching down the centreline. This in turn will create resistance from your opponent which you use to accelerate the punch off your centre when pulling it. This makes it harder for your partner to recover with their own 'Bong Sao' deflection if they apply too much aggressive force to their punch.

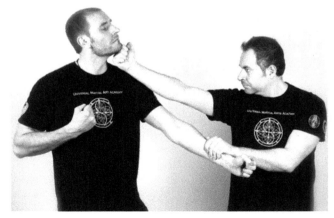

This drill sequence offers an excellent way for you to build up fast response and reflex to quick changes and flowing structures. The tempo and power used in the exercise should be constantly changed so the practitioners do not become robotic when performing it. The structures used in this drill should be constantly challenged for correct positioning and flow, it feels alive and real as you challenge each other for position.

There are several changes that can be implemented also into the exercise. For instance, as the Wu Sao structure is applied to the punching arm, the fist of the punching arm turns into a Lap Sao and pulls the Wu Sao across the centre, forcing it into a Bong Sao deflection. This causes a change of arm positions.

Another way is to change the Lap Sao into a straight punch, which forces the training partner to change their Wu Sao into a Bong Sao deflection, rotating through Kwun Sao and again, changing your positions.

It is important to mention that the elbow on the punching arm should only straighten if it gets through, if and the force of the punch should always be pressing out from the ground. If applied correctly, it will not force the deflection in Bong Sao and will not offer the opponent a gap to strike underneath it, the punch will simply arrive at your centre, where its energy will focus forward while sticking to the prying Bong

Sao. Also, prying force between the two training partners should be constant through out the movements. The feeling in Bong Sao is like leaning against a wall with the contact point being the elbow, the shoulder is relaxed and the body is supported by the upper arm humorous bone.

If the Bong Sao is pulled down at the wrist, the Bong Sao moves to the low position, Dai Bong Sao, you will arrive at the Kwun Sao again, defending the low line with Dai Bong, and the high line with Tan Sao. If you resist a pulling down action, you strain your shoulder and are hit easily.

If your Bong Sao is pressed down at the elbow by the training partners punching arm, it should flow into Tan Sao and Tan Da is applied, you have changed arms.

If the Wu Sao is pulled straight down by the training partner, you should not fight it and attempt to lift your Bong, instead, step forward and thrust your shoulder at their centre.

When the Lap Sao is applied to you, always try to outrun the action using Huen Sao so you can thrust the Fak Sao forward at the throat.

Single Sticking Hands/Dan Chi Sao

Once the exercise of Teng Sao is well understood, we develop the sharp angle of attack and deflection through the form and specific bridging exercises, that require the practitioners to keep arms in contact and develop the feeling further with an emphasis on economical attack and counter attacking actions. The primary exercise is Dan Chi Sao. This single arm exercise attempts to teach the correct feeling, intent and reaction to the opponent's arm when in contact with you. You should feel your entire body is behind the actions that are constantly focused forwards and level at the partners' chest. Only pressing up, down or to the sides, when forcing a change of positions. During this exercise you should remain balanced, in 'Yee Jee Kim Yuen Ma' and square on to your partner at all times.

We train the response to incoming force using the Tan/Jeung/Jum/Jin Choi, Bong Sao deflections and strikes.

This drill can be practiced at a number of ranges, either with the wrists of the structures in contact, or with the contact further down the forearms and nearer the elbows. You can also alternate with one at short and one at long range.

Once the movements are understood, the sequence can become more live, with many changes in angle of the attacking and deflecting movements, forced changes in positioning, flowing and later, stepping and turning can also be applied. Once the basic principles of this drill are understood, with all the correct prying forces applied, we can begin to practice the exercise with flowing structures and footwork that can be used to bring the exercise to life. All structures can now be used with turning and stepping, which begins to teach you how to recover the line of attack if forced into a diverting movement. At this stage of training the emphasis is on flowing with pressure while retaining focused force back at the opponents centre line.

Some examples of changes in application during the drill are as follows. When performing the palm strike, you can rotate your torso to extend the striking range. You can take it further by stepping forward with the palm strike, stepping forward while rotating the torso also, or adding a leaning forward stance to give it even greater range. In all these instances, they develop greater understanding in the responding Sinking Arm/Jum Sao counter structure, which should now be very heavy in application.

Training for good reflex reaction while maintaining the guard, exploring ranges, developing bridging and flowing energy cultivation, springing force resistance, stance and footwork.

Double sticking Arms/Seung Chi Sao

This exercise connects both arms of the practitioners together. Seung Chi Sao introduces the double arm rolling. Seung Chi Sao is similar to the Dan Chi Sao exercise, except the counter response to the punch is to pry forward with Tan Sao instead of deflecting with a Bong Sao. While one side of the arms are practiced, the other side bridge and press against each other forming a solid structure which remains perfectly static. Once the moving structures have been performed, Dai Jeung, countered with Jum Sao, then Jic Chung Choi, countered with a prying Tan Sao, the arms are rolled and the sequence is practiced on the other side.

This exercise can have stepping footwork added to it to further develop the idea of receiving force and correcting posture when uprooted or riding the opponent's bridges. With the correct prying force applied, minimal movement should be required to create the deflection of prying forces. When performing the striking actions in this exercise, you should only be moving about an inch before you feel your strike is being successfully deflected, if you move any further forward after that, you should feel vulnerable to your partners counter and aware of your elbow being poorly positioned.

If your partners structures are incorrect, you should be able to hit with ease, at which point, you should point out their mistakes so they can fix their defences.

Rolling Arms/Poon Sao/Luk Sao

Rolling with prying, punching force. This exercise begins to develop free rolling, changing structures, being mobile in the arms while remaining guarded by the elbows and forearms. It also develops the ability to move around strong positions while keeping the elbows firmly connected to pressure and therefore not offering the partner any room to advance. Force from the floor is constantly pressed out between the training partners and is absorbed into the floor through the arm structures. Effectively, both training partners are pressing each other into the ground. Strong pressing force is a constant feature in this exercise. At this stage of training, this exercise should be practiced in a static position. When rolling, try to pulse striking force into the end of each rolling action, this will begin to develop the correct striking responses and forward rush when the opponents defence fails.

Once the basic idea is understood, direct stimulus is also given by the training partners to deliberately force structures to collapse, learning how to flow into the next best structure and to flow around pressing force when it is incorrectly applied to regain the centre-line.

Listening Hands/Teng Sao

From the exercise of 'Listening Hands', we learn how to deal with free flowing force being applied to the arms and body through light pushing, pressing and yielding. This energy is given and taken from both partners in the exercise. Through this exercise the players therefore learn to redirect force by feeling it directly applied through connected arms. Once relaxed connection is felt and understood it can be used to manipulate the opposing players balance and root. When we uproot our opponent, we can drive all power from our stance and waist into the counter attack and at the same time, prevent our opponent from countering with rooted force.

Once the very fundamental stance is understood, we extend the energy from the feet and waist into the arms, specifically the elbows, wrists and hands and meditate on keeping it in our partners centre of mass and develop random pushing, pulling, pressing and leading hands skills. It begins slowly so you can build a true sense of feeling resistance. As your skill improves, you will get faster and faster and able to apply huge forces on one another while maintaining balance.

The game is to make your partner move out of their rooted stance. When one of your feet moves off its spot, reset and begin again. Any tactic can be used as long as it does not involve striking, the idea is to train your stance and body structure to be strong yet flexible while controlling your partners balance, arms and legs.

I can feel your energy, therefore I know your intention, if I oppose you in any direction, your energy will shift from centre in the opposite direction. You can now be hit without obstruction. Understand this and you can apply many angles, structures and techniques to achieve the same goal, knocking out the attacker. Flow to find the centre, keep your knees, waist and elbow in mind!

Begin in and remain square on to your training partner. Learn to use the stance square on to avoid offering an extended leg, as in combat it may be kicked. Keep your energy in the waist and feel it connect to the elbows. Whenever you need to turn, use the waist to lead the elbows and keep the energy connected, you will then be able to use torque, manifesting in the elbows, and able to lever heavy force if it is offered to you. Whenever your opponent attempts to turn you however, you must disconnect this energy once you feel a firm commitment from your opponent, allow them to lose your centre while you take theirs.

When forced to be soft, be soft, when you can fight hard, fight hard! If you do step forward, take the centre, lock the opponent's knee or stand on their foot.

With the listening hands skills understood at this basic level, there is a real ability to competently and powerfully connect to an incoming strike and bring it under control or deflect it away from your centre. Importantly, at this stage we have learned to bring the attacker to us while preventing them from striking, through clinching to their arms and feeling their stance, we work with the intention of lining our force up to disrupt and take the opponents balance, by manipulating their arms, torso and waist.

If you loose your balance when fighting, you loose your ability to strike back with the stance driving the energy into the elbow, "the piston", you have therefore lost the moment to attack.

Although this is not the end of the world, moving back has its place, but it can create problems if you have a very committed attacker. As you move back, you get lighter and they get heavier. If you take one step back, immediately side step to regain alignment to their centre and force them into a rotation, this puts the opponent in a vulnerable position if their attacking stance is narrow, as it leads them into a crossed arm position.

Once these levels have been trained thoroughly, you can now stand your ground and fight hard. At this point, counter footwork is practiced, first to learn to drive the body weight forward behind the elbow, then by side stepping incoming structures and simply lining up our shots.

With footwork trained and understood, we have a natural, powerful and flowing fighting style. We now concentrate on developing the striking actions that come from the primary defensive positions in Bong/Tan/Fook Sao and how all the other actions in form connect together in a free flow exercise to develop efficient attack while maintaining defence. Teng Sao is rounded, softer, with focus on spiralling energy.

Sticking Hands/Chi Sao

This exercise allows the training partners to freely express the structures learned in the forms and all other exercises which adapt to the method of attack being applied. Control is exercised and whenever an attempt to strike is countered or deflected, methods are analysed as to how to effectively pass the defence. When the defence is passed, the problem of how to create a defence against the next strike is looked at. When our defensive positions are constantly exploited, weaknesses in defence are gradually rectified so control of the centre-line is strong, fluid and constant.

You should practice with full co-operation so it does not become a competition in the mind of the training partners and an utter waste of time. If the two practitioners are highly skilled, it can be a highly stimulating exercise, with multiple attacking and defensive techniques and rapid changes of direction being constantly fired at each other. It is impossible to avoid striking each other all the time, but control should be in the forefront of your mind always.

The Chi Sao exercise has thousands of potential problems and solutions, attacks and counterattacks that can be presented and overcome by diligent practice. But you should always keep the techniques within the basic guidelines of the system, do not try anything impractical or inefficient. It should always be the basic, fast and efficient techniques that you employ in this exercise. In training, practicing partners confer with each other and advise on the strengths and weaknesses they are feeling in each other. Constant correction closes all the gaps and makes defence efficient and effective. The ability to meet force and redirect it smoothly from your centre line while simultaneously striking the opponents centre is at the heart of its practice.

With all of the concepts discussed in this book present, your Chi Sao will feel powerful, yet fluid, threatening yet controlled. The mind focuses on the opponents centre of mass, intent drives the energy through the body structure, the body structure supports the elbow, which guides the forearm and hand which feel flexible and spongy.

Chi Sao is angular, using energy in the elbows to flex into the wrists in order to stop an attacking arm, with force that attacks the opponents centre immediately on contact. When the wrists of the lead hand move or are moved off centre, the elbow of that arm will keep centre, as in moving from a punch to a Bong Sao.

Bong Sao is utilised as a secondary defensive position should you overextend your punch. However, if you continue to drive the elbow forward, it becomes a striking elbow. If not extending the elbow forward to strike, it may be used to draw the energy back into the waist.

While the waist turns and draws the elbow back towards the hip, it pulls the forearm which in turn pulls the wrist and hand, bringing it back into position.

In Chin Na, these actions can also be used to control and apply or counter joint manipulation. The Bong Sao here is also called the 'Universal Angle'. This angle is felt for constantly during practice. If the elbow rises above the shoulder line it can be accelerated over the opponents head, destroying their balance and root. From there it can be manipulated into a numbers of painful locks. Going further, the universal angle is also applied to the fingers and toes, as in small joint manipulation.

In Chi Sao we are training to extend the energy of the stance, from the waist, into the elbows, wrists and hands dynamically. Training partners offer resistance that allows you to train for the correct feeling. When the bridging force meets, it should be equal between the players. The stance should be maintained, allow the force of your arms in contact, to press you into further into the floor, until you feel sprung, your legs ready to propel you forwards if your partners energy is suddenly removed. This same energy will propel your arm into a strike if your partners arm drops away. The drill has no end of techniques of flow to learn, create and apply.

Sticky Legs/Chi Gurk

When legs are pressing at each other, look to control the knee. If your opponent presses forward onto your knee, you can counter by circling your knee and press theirs to the side. If they press your knee to the side, you can counter by coming around their knee and then pressing it from the front. If you can bend forward and press your knee very low to the ground you will be able to make the opponent fall. This can also be achieved by sweeping their foot, either backwards or to the sides. In practice, it adds another element to Chi Sao and gives a more complete ability to defend high with the hands, and low with the legs.

Random Hands. San Sao/Gor Sao

Once you are comfortable with the structures in the forms, if you practice the sequences, how they work and how to apply them make your training more realistic.

In this exercise, vary the angles of attack, striking at the head, torso and groin in order to train the correct response as well as changing the speed and frequency of your attacking actions.

Separate hands exercises train to get your reaction speed and timing to a high level. You are training for correct response to stimulus, getting the correct feel for range, timing, deflecting energy, inch force, absorption, redirection, sticking, yielding, swallowing, lifting, pulling, pressing, slipping and striking, learning to also deal with range when attacked by kicks and long weapons as well as contact range from grappling. When performing Separate Hands/San Sao, you should not signal your intent to the training partner, attack as fast as you can and vary the methods of your attack to see how they cope. Over time, your reactions become sharper and you are able to co-ordinate hand positions, body power, footwork and timing, and you will have the ability to deal with most methods of attack successfully and in a controlled and immediate way.

Joint Manipulation/Kum Na/Chin Na

The methods of grappling upright and on the ground should be trained as a natural extension of fight training. Sometimes when advancing your strike may miss, you may get too close to the opponent to strike freely or may crash into each other. You should train to be comfortable in this scenario. When you practice you should slowly stretch your partner to the extremes of their tolerance, and have them do the same to you, you gain even more flexibility and power.

Small joint manipulation on fingers and wrists, large joint manipulation to the elbows, shoulder, neck and back. When training, always train to strike before moving into a joint lock, stun the opponent first and then break the limb or control and restrain the opponent.

Learn how to move on the floor, when on your back and when on top of the opponent. Also train to get to your feet as quickly as possible, remember, in a situation on the street there may be more than one attacker to deal with.

Final Thoughts

Martial arts primarily offer advice and guidance on how best to deal with aggression and violence. One method or system will suit an individual more than another, due to the size, strength and physical and mental ability of that individual practitioner. The length of time training in a system is also a major factor in its successful application. Some techniques may only be successfully applied after many years of practice, while other techniques may work immediately. All styles offer a method of attaining high levels of fighting/self defence skill, but some offer a more direct way of learning than others.

Many people I have met in training over the years all have the same response when you ask them why they began classes, 'self defence'. Yet when they are training, they hardly break a sweat. If the reason you are training is to learn to protect yourself, training must be undertaken in earnest. Someone intending to do you harm and physically moving in at you in an aggressive and threatening way, should always be dealt with quickly and ruthlessly. They go down, and you go home. An aggressor that attacks you with a weapon is not play fighting, so you must be very serious in your response, especially if they appear competent in their movement. If you hesitate, you risk the potential of permanent disability or death. The greater their threat, the greater and more serious your response should be, this you will learn from the start of your training, but as the years pass, the reasons for continued practice can change.

Martial arts are ultimately a science of harmony. In training we move towards the harmonious state, one day at a time. You may be an angry, uptight, aggressive individual when you begin your journey, but the better you get, the calmer and more confident your mood will become. Achieving a level of competency in your chosen system, will develop a capable body and mind. A capable body and mind will allow you to relax, relaxing will reduce stress, reduced stress will reduce anxiety and fear and so peace and harmony will permeate your being. You should approach the martial arts with a sense of calm and recognise that when learning, you are not in competition with your class mates and training partners.

To progress quickly in a chosen skill, open up to the idea of sharing information and doing your utmost to help the system and those that practice it, evolve productively. Martial artists of any system should realise that, we are not striving to beat each other and to be segregated, martial arts should be used as a way to come together, to share information that will make us all productive, strong and outstanding members of society. We do not learn these skills so we can impose our will on others, we learn these skills to protect ourselves, friends, loved ones and strangers in need.

If you are so inclined, you can compete, fight and gain recognition in this arena but to do this, you learn to fight within a set of rules.

Populist modern day sport martial arts like 'Mixed Martial Arts' work in the competitive arena because they have rules of engagement, and are a sport in which healthy strong athletes can compete and gain an identity. It deals with common methods of attack and trains many facets of physical combat, being great for fitness and a positive mental attitude. This is a positive for many young people and one that should be encouraged. Systems like Wing Chun are not a sport. Some skills are designed and practiced purely for self defence and some for when the situation is 'serious'. Whatever you choose to practice, be sure to understand the differences between each.

You should feel relaxed when in class and see your fellow practitioners as friends and do your best to help the less experienced in a way that helps them to relax and trust you. Class time is for study and practice, you are not winning and losing when training drills or the forms applications. An attitude for "winning," is fine when you compete, spar and definitely when you fight, but the time spent in class, you and all those around you are there to learn the detail of the system.

Improvement in positioning, reflex reaction, energy, instinct, hand eye co-ordination, relaxed application of body structure and striking power, execution of principles in form are all assets that are part of your personal development in martial arts training. Your fellow practitioners should all be willing to help you, explain the finer points in what they are doing and share advice, and also display a slightly different idea to their classmates, that they have developed when learning and practicing for themselves. It is important that you make it work for you, which will require you to adapt certain concepts or applications based on your physical stature and ability.

A good teacher will watch you, correct you and share what they know to improve you as much as they can, giving guidance based on your level of understanding and ability. You should feel you can ask them a sensible question but whether you will understand what they tell you or be able to apply it in practice will also reflect your level of understanding at that time. Take your time to absorb information, do not rush yourself, it is better to know one technique well, than ten techniques you cannot apply.

Seeing things in training for the first time can be overwhelming. Re-thinking how you apply yourself, your physical and mental energy can seem a little "out there". Give yourself the time to learn, it's not a race, it's a journey. The reasons you come to learn a martial art will change over time, but every day should involve some level of improvement.

The system is showing you a framework that you apply your mind and physical body to. There is huge diversity in technique and so many more methods, tactics concepts and applications. All the movements explained in this book show you methods within this framework, and offer you a certain concept. However, the system is much more than this book, there are many millions of people practicing this in their own way, focusing on the ideas that work for them, developing myriad combination of technique and concept, and developing them to a high level. They are all out there, figuring it out. My advice, try and get around to meet some of them, you will learn a lot more. As time passes I believe more and more people will come to realise this, and the younger students will embrace a multi dimensional approach to learning, one based on fact in application no matter what the source. It will take a lifetime to know them all, but like the taste of a fine wine, your skill will improve with age.

In conclusion, I would like to remind you that these are just a few of the many variations on technique that can be applied, but just learning the skills outlined in this book, can take many years to learn, and many more to apply. I hope you have enjoyed reading this book as much as I have writing it. It has been very challenging, arranging my thoughts in an order that makes the most sense to me when teaching this amazing system.

I hope this book has given you some new ideas for training and will go on to improve what you do and that your life is filled with happiness, health and joy.

Good luck in all you do.

Sifu Jason G Kokkorakis.

About the Author

I began studying martial arts in 1982. Beginning with Judo, and then moving onto Wu Shu Kwan and Tai Chi. After several years practicing Wu Shu Kwan, in 1986 I moved with my family to Portugal. At that time, having no one to train with, I continued my training regime as it had been taught to me by my first teacher.

Mr Ho, had a martial arts shop in the indoor market in Croydon, and I would spend as much time as I could there, learning whatever I could. Under his guidance, I learned the balisong, escrima and nunchuku. I also got to practice knife and stick drills with him when the shop was quiet, which was great. I was a thirteen year old kid that got to hang around with his master. At that time I also attended his Wu Shu Kwan classes on a monday and wednesday night and worked hard on my kicking techniques as often as possible. As I grew and got stronger and heavier I sparred more and more, and was lucky that my best friend, Andrew Lieu had moved up the ranks to Black Belt in Kyokushinkai Karate under Sensei Levi Pedie, an Instructor under Greg Wallace. We were kids, fifteen or sixteen years old. Andy "Ming" and I would get together and exchange what we were learning at every opportunity, generally knocking each other about on a weekly basis.

After the move to Portugal and making friends there, word of my passion for the martial arts spread and I began to get to know other practitioners, one in Capoeira. What a great style, I loved it, as it offered variations of application from what I had been learning. Joe, was a 22 year old Dj from Brazil and the Capoeira expert, whose grandfather had taught him back home. Our first training session resulted in Joe literally beating me up with style. After that experience I knew I had only scratched the surface in training terms and began to look further. Joe immediately inspired me to drop the ego and open my eyes. I continued to practice everything I had learned in the UK and began to research other systems at that time from any source I could find. I worked, I trained, I went to nightclubs, got drunk and after the hangover, I trained some more. No internet back then, no youtube, just books and other people to fight and train with.

By 1991, back in the UK, I enrolled in college and made friends with some great guys that were into Boxing and Kickboxing. Pedro Acha, Marc Golland and I used to get together regularly for training sessions. Pedro and I also began classes in Aikido under Sensei Paul Chambers. Over time our training circles grew, making friends in Ju Jitsu, Tae Kwon Do, Escrima and Boxing. This training was almost daily and continued for the duration of my time at college. We then all got our places at different Universities and moved away.

Once at Oxford I immediately enrolled in an Aikido class Sensei Paul had recommended. This was with Sensei Kanetsuka and Sensei Peter Megan. Sensei Kanetsuke was a small man with a mastery of leverage and pressure points. I got stuck into practice. Pedro meanwhile in Leeds had began Wing Chun Classes.

Still studying Aikido, I also began attending classes in Wudang Tai Chi Chuan under Dave Baker and Kendo under Sensei Peter Wells. At

University, word of my martial arts enthusiasm spread, and I was invited to teach self defence classes in the University campus leisure facility alongside Sensei Nora Mukachung. Training with Pedro in Wing Chun soon got me along to where he was learning and there I met Sifu Colin Ward. At my first class I was 22. At that age its hard to take a 15 year old seriously as a threat, but that was my first training partner. "Attack him anyway you want and see how he responds" was the challenge from Sifu; I backed up to throw a kick the kid grabbed my arms and stuck to me, and every time I moved it seemed, he hit me, and I couldn't do anything about it. That was it, I was hooked, and drove to Leeds as often as possible to learn. But better still, Pedro and I could now discuss the system on the phone when we could not train together, and it became a talking point that we could spend hours on, we were learning Ip Chun Wing Chun.

While still training in all the other disciplines in Oxford, at Wudang Tai Chi I met Eddie Yuen. A retired tai chi martial arts expert, I think at the time he just didn't know it. His Tai Chi was great, and his enthusiasm for Wing Chun was infectious. We began training together and others joined our group, we often trained together. During that time Eddie had contacted Sifu Nino Bernardo for instruction and suggested I contact Sifu Clive Potter to do the same. We could then train together and share the technical information we were learning from these Sifu.

Due to finances, Aikido and Kendo practice had to come to an end. I also stopped teaching and studying at the University, left my law degree behind and began to focus more on my personal Wing Chun and Tai Chi training. During that time in Oxford I was traveling to St Albans for lessons and having private tuition as often as I could afford it. I then had the opportunity to move to Greece and catch up with family I had not seen in many years and so once again I moved abroad to stay in my fathers empty apartment.

Soon after my arrival I met up with several other Wing Chun teachers from different lineages. My father's apartment was not a good setting for training, so we went on the rooftops to train there. During that time I started training with a Sifu under Master Duncan Leung, that was Sifu Frank Grispos. After a short time, I began working out of his studio and trained with him and his students. We also trained Kali there.

By that time I had also began learning some Gracie Ju Jitsu techniques from one of my students and his instructor and also met and trained with Sifu Michael Papadonakis formerly under Sifu William Cheung. Living in Greece was not for me and so I returned to the UK at the end of 1999. Since then, I have thrown myself further into Wing Chun training. I have studied and practiced the system daily, analysing every piece of video footage, book and article I could find from all the varied methods, concepts and applications. Andrew Lieu became a Sensei in Karate, Pedro Acha became a Sifu under Colin Ward, Marc Golland now owns and runs the Guildford academy of martial arts and Eddie Yuen became a Sifu under Nino Bernado.

I now run the Lincoln Ip Man Ving Tsun Academy and train, teach classes, workshops and one to one sessions full time. Some of my students and I have attended seminars with Sifu David Peterson, Sifu Nino Bernado and GrandMaster Samuel Kwok. I have also arranged workshops at my school with Sifu Benny Meng and Sifu Cheung Kwok Chow and Alan Gibson and in 2012 was certified by Grandmaster

Samuel Kwok, and also given the Chinese name "Flying Dragon", a great honour.

To contact me please visit my website at www.umaa.org.uk or join me on Facebook.